Metateaching and the Instructional Map

by William M. Timpson

Atwood Publishing
Madison, Wisconsin

Metateaching and the Instructional Map
by William M. Timpson

Volume 1, Teaching Techniques/Strategies Series
Atwood Publishing

© 1999
Atwood Publishing
2710 Atwood Ave.
Madison, WI 53704

Printed in the United States of America.

02 01 00 99 9 8 7 6 5 4 3 2 1

Cover design © 1999
by Tamara L. Dever, TLC Graphics

Timpson, William M.
    Metateaching and the instructional map/by William M. Timpson. Includes bibliographical reference (p.) and index.
    ISBN 1-891859-29-3
    1. Teaching. 2. Metacognition. 3. Maps in education. I. Title. II. Series.
LB1025.3.T56   1999
371.3—dc21   99-16524
                                                              CIP

Dedication

To the stars we need for navigation
Compass points for our work, dreams,
and explorations

table of contents

foreword

BY
PARKER PALMER

For the past fifteen or twenty years, I have been making the case that good teaching can never be reduced to technique. I do not mean that technique is irrelevant — I mean that reducing good teaching to the moves we make is far too simplistic to capture the nuances of our demanding art and craft.

Good teaching comes, I believe, from a complex and mysterious source: from the identity and integrity of the teacher as it interacts with the nature of one's discipline and the nature of the students one is teaching. As we come to understand our own identity better, we can learn techniques that help us reveal — rather than conceal — who we are, techniques that help us hold both our knowledge and our students in ways that are life-giving for them and for us.

This is a hard case to make in a culture that likes to "keep things simple" by turning every issue it faces into a technical problem whose solution can be found in the method du jour. So it has been a real joy for me to discover the work that Bill Timpson has done on teaching. His writing occupies that wonderful middle ground between the Procrustean bed of technique and theoretical abstractions about teaching and learning that offer no practical guidance.

This is especially true of his new book, *Metateaching and the Instructional Map*, in which he offers a tool to help us explore issues that all teachers face. "Map" is the perfect metaphor for the approach to teaching we need. When we set out on an adventure — which real teaching is — we do not want to be told where to go or how to get there; that sort of guidance turns an adventure into a forced march that is both predictable and boring. But we do want a good map of the territory — one that shows distances, directions, elevations, and types of terrain — so that the choices we make as we travel can be made knowingly.

That is what Bill Timpson's new book offers to all of us who teach. Without telling us what we are supposed to do or how we are supposed to do it — for the only true answers to those questions require a complex computation of self, subject, and students — Timpson's map allows us to reflect both creatively and self-critically on the journey called teaching, from its outset in a course design, through issues of implementation, to its conclusion in student learning.

Bill Timpson has more than a map to offer. As this book makes abundantly clear, he loves teaching, he loves learning, and he loves people who teach and learn. That is the most important qualification for anyone who sets out to teach teachers. Read his book and deepen your love for this life-giving art and craft as well as your competence.

Parker Palmer
1999

passages AND pathfinders

BY
GAILMARIE KIMMEL

I can remember clearly how struck I was by the biographical-like descriptions in Gail Sheehy's book, *Passages* — how accurate her depictions seemed to be of the stages of my own life, what I was going through. It felt eerie, so close to the mark. Dan Levinson's *Seasons of a Man's Life* was just as telling. So it was with great interest that I picked up Sheehy's follow-up work, *Pathfinders,* to see how she profiled leaders, trendsetters, and risk takers. How would teachers fare? Would Sheehy's work offer any insights through that maze of interactive variables characterizing instruction — that intersection of teacher, content, students, and physical space?

In Chapter One of the book, Sheehy offered a brief review of her research (1976, 22):

> One of the most striking similarities among blue-collar, white-collar, and professional groups included in my research is that the five self-descriptions most closely linked to well-being were identical in all. Their importance even ranked in the same order:
>
> 1. My life has meaning and direction.
>
> 2. I have experienced one or more important transitions in my adult years, and I have handled these transitions in an unusual, personal, or creative way.
>
> 3. I rarely feel cheated or disappointed by life.
>
> 4. I have already attained several of the long-term goals that are important to me.
>
> 5. I am pleased with my personal growth and development.

As I reviewed this list, I noted the references to direction and goals as well as the inferred connections to attitude and learning.

As teachers, we have the challenging task of leading diverse groups of students down paths that are intended to produce understanding of new ideas and mastery of new skills. What is clear to me from Sheehy's work is that to foster deep learning, we need a clear sense of direction, a vision that has meaning for us personally, confidence in ourselves and a commitment to lifelong growth, faith in our students, an optimism about our work, determination to overcome whatever obstacles might appear, and a cheerfulness about it all — worthwhile reminders for any endeavor.

A *map* can help us keep all of these requirements together and in perspective.

Gailmarie Kimmel is a senior staff member in the Division of Educational Outreach as well as an instructor in education at Colorado State University.

introduction

Have you ever been lost when you're teaching, uncomfortable with a rambling discussion dominated by only a few students? Have you ever gotten so far into the subtleties of your own areas of expertise that your students lost sight of the main points you were trying to make? Do you shy away from having students work in small groups because you believe that having them do so would take time away from covering content? Have you ever ventured out from the "tried and true" only to be confused by the new terrain?

If you answered "yes" to any of these questions, maybe a guide would help — and so I offer you the *Instructional Map*.

As a teacher, you make countless decisions in every class session: what to say and how, when to pause and ask for responses, how to respond to whatever student diversity you face (the range of personalities, backgrounds, motivations, preparation, and values), how to keep students engaged, what tangents to pursue, when to review, when to move on, how much to turn over to discussion, what to emphasize, what depth and breadth to seek, what the limits are on your own knowledge. The options seem endless — an evolving, complex, dynamic intersection of multiple variables and, often, competing forces.

At any point you could follow a number of different paths. In *Metateaching and the Instructional Map* I describe a conceptual framework that can help you keep the mix of variables before you as you plan, as you sort your way through course material and your various options for instruction, as you interact with students in and out of class, and as you step back to reflect upon progress made and what remains to be done.

Think of the *Instructional Map* as a compass you can use when you get lost or when you're out exploring new terrain. Very simply, the *Instructional Map* is a way to think about your teaching across three distinct continua:

1. From a *teacher-directed* approach (lecture, presentation) to one that is more *student-centered* (practice, discussion-based).

2. From a focus on *product* (knowledge, skills) to a focus on *process* (critical and creative thinking, communicating, cooperating).

3. From an *individual* context to a *group* context (small, large, or whole class).

Working with others — e.g., other teachers or even students — and using the *Instructional Map* can give you a common language to share concerns, discuss ideas, explore innovations, and evaluate improvements. It can help remind you of the interconnectedness of teaching and learning — for example, the ways students think about the content, or the effect of student engagement on your own attitudes and emotions. In the midst of all the decisions you must make with respect to content and process, here is a way to step back periodically and reassess your place in the larger picture.

By helping you plot the intersection of course content and learning objectives with whatever activities you have planned, the *Instructional Map* can give you a useful outline. As such, it can provide both conceptual and visual cues for short- and long-range planning, for reflection and review, and for thinking through individual lessons or an entire course. It can also serve as a systematic check while you are teaching, a convenient reminder of what you still want to do given the time remaining in any particular class period.

As I have worked with the *Instructional Map*, its value has evolved for me. Initially it helped mostly to provide a visual framework for everything I wanted to do during a particular class period, as well as helpful reminders once class began. Then I found that the *Map* had value as a reference for review, to help me reflect back and compare what *did* happen with what I had *wanted* to happen. Over time, I also found the *Map* useful for helping me illustrate to students the various concepts or strategies I used, which helped me make my teaching more "transparent," my expectations more clear. In essence, the *Map* has helped me stand above or outside of instructional planning, delivery, and review to see more of the whole picture, content and process — an act I call *metateaching*.

I wrote this book to share the concept of the *Instructional Map* with you.

In the first portion of the book, I describe the *Instructional Map* and how it can help you think more systematically about your teaching, your goals for student learning, getting students to be more critical and creative, and balancing what you present with what you want in the way of active student participation. Gailmarie Kimmel describes her use of mapping to help students better orient themselves to the campus, to the values of the academic community, and to the resources that can support their learning. I also offer a brief overview of the *Instructional Map* and its varied uses, as well as some thoughts about cartography, mapping, and orienteering in general.

In the next section of the book I touch on parallel work — such as *concept mapping* and Ausubel's *advance organizer* — drawing on Gagné's classic work on learning, rules, and higher-order rules as well as Perry's research on cognitive development. I go on to discuss *metacognition*, or thinking about thinking, and my own concept of *metateaching* — how stepping back from your teaching can help you get more perspective, the big picture. Teaching is an intensely complex intersection of individuals, content, and place. As a teacher, you are judge and jury, planner and evaluator, presenter and motivator, facilitator and guide, taskmaster and friend. The list goes on.

In the next portion, I explain the *Instructional Map* in greater detail and offer still other uses for it. Next, I describe how the *Instructional Map* can be used to provide useful feedback to teachers and students — assessments that can serve well as a basis for conversations about instruction and learning. Finally, I offer a number of examples in which I use the *Instructional Map* to give you brief overviews of different approaches to teaching.

Hopefully, you will also appreciate and enjoy the quotations sprinkled throughout the text — thoughts about maps and direction and teaching, from a variety of my favorite sources.

So enjoy. And if you do get lost, you now have a guide and some choices. You can use the *Instructional Map* to help find your way back home. Or you can use it to settle your nerves and enjoy more of that strange new terrain you've been waiting to explore.

CHAPTER I

Of Story and Journey, Map and place

by Gailmarie Kimmel

One drawer of my desk is stuffed with all kinds of maps — from sturdy *National Geographic* inserts to the taped-and-tattered remains of a map tracing the lesser-known temples of Bangkok. I never quite convince myself to recycle any of these maps on the off chance I recommend that lovely trail outside of Banff, need a "Best in the West" thrift store in Denver, opt for jade on Canton Street, or crave a "natural sauna" in Helsinki.

I cherish maps. They help me navigate though the richness of nature and culture as they clue me into real stories and expand my own. (And, as you will hear, "mapping" is a wonderful teaching tool, lending itself easily to metaphor and creativity.) The idea of an *Instructional Map* is, therefore, appealing and practical to me. It has guided me through the endless possibilities of material, participation, and optimal learning.

Let me share with you a recent example. Recently, the author of this book, Bill Timpson, and I taught an experimental course for incoming first-year university students whose predictors indicated that many of them were "academically at risk." Among the forty-six students were undeclared "open option" students, students with learning disabilities, and probationary students. Working toward the general goal of fostering students' self-awareness as learners and members of learning communities, I was primarily concerned with helping orient them to three such communities — the campus, the town, and the Front Range of Colorado — so that they could begin establishing a sense of home here.

Inspired by Paul Devereux's book, *Reinventing the Earth*, I invented exercises to enliven student awareness as they explored stories of learning and community. Three of the book's themes — placing, journeying, and mapping — promised to foster an interconnectedness with all of life while deepening each student's sense of identity.

Bill and I moved fluidly along the three instructional continua (teacher-centered to student-centered, individual to group, and content to participation) as outlined in this book. In the end, we were delighted to see young people navigating the transition to college with more ease and confidence — oh, and better grades as well! Here are some of the highlights:

Placing

Early on, I asked students to introduce themselves using their "Earth Address" — by citing the dominant land or water form of the place they called home and adding a personal descriptor. Their responses included: "Powerful Pacific," "Boring plains," "Majestic forest," and "Peaceful beaches." Not surprisingly, dramatic landscapes and oceans fared better than the seemingly more uniform features of deserts, plains, and city parks.

Then, to help the students begin exploring their new natural environment, I assigned a solo exploration of the Poudre River, our local natural treasure and a ten-minute bike ride from campus. To stimulate the students' imaginations, I told historical stories of how the river got its name and of the river's relationship to local Indian tribes and European settlers. I even led a guided visualization on the concept of watershed, following the Poudre's journey as it navigated from the high Rockies to the Gulf of Mexico, and drawing parallels to the students' own journeys of growth and adventure.

I instructed the students to experience twenty minutes of silent walking or sitting by the river and to then briefly query one or two people along the path to learn about *their* "river time." Many of the ensuing reflections were touching. Solitude is not a modern birthright but, rather, something people choose to befriend, usually only with some maturity. Indeed, most students documented their own resistance to the assignment. And yet they were grateful for the quiet time away from the residence halls, for the opportunity to find a place within themselves for some peace and perspective, and for the introduction to an easy, cheap treat beyond campus. The Poudre was becoming a part of their new Earth Address.

Journeying

Combining a scavenger hunt with a stroll down memory lane, I developed a list of campus locations for students to find on their walk to visit our city's museum, which is about twenty minutes from campus. I emphasized history — for example, the Vietnam Memorial Bridge, the turn-of-the-century photographs decorating the food court, the historic and current administration buildings, and the remains from the 1970 burning of Old Main. At the city museum, the students toured the one-room schoolhouse (known to them only from the movies) and viewed the mementos of times past "out west." Again, many of their reflections were noteworthy. Some definitely felt the imprint of previous generations of young dreamers, college-bound and not, and returned to campus feeling a bit more at home along this well-traveled western path.

Mapping

I issued a creative challenge to the students: create a 24-inch-by-36-inch collage of their life in the form of a line, linking life events with geography and time. The overall structure of their life maps took many forms, from a mandala spiraling out to a road map adventure to a meandering stream growing into a river. Memorabilia from home, magazine cutouts, computer graphics, and artwork helped the maps come alive. The maps started with the students' birthdates and ended at college. As one student commented, "I'd never really thought about my life this way before." Exactly.

In order to create a panel that would come immediately before their own lifelines, I then asked the students to explore the lives of their parents and grandparents, plotting the geography of their family members' life events, residences, relationships, travels, and occupations. A mixed discussion resulted. Few students knew their family tree well, so our questions seemed to prompt some curiosity and investment in the stories that had shaped them. Some heard the stories of diversity that were hidden beneath their earlier surface impressions of their classmates. Other students realized how unique their own stories were, perhaps seeing their lineage with new depth and appreciation. Many acted detached from their own family stories but listened intently to other students' narratives. Hopefully,

I planted some important seeds in this activity — or, rather, considering the students' places among the branches of their family trees, some awareness of roots, growth rings, and seasons past.

Finally, I asked the students to discuss the panel coming after their present lifelines: their future. I encouraged them to explore the geography of their goals and dreams, mapping out time frames and optimal routes for achieving them. This drew more engaged conversations. These young people were very concerned about their futures and eager to find clarity and inspiration.

Integration

For the grand finale of our fifteen weeks together, the students walked the "Walk through Deep Time," a large spiral of rope chronicling the 15 billion or so years through evolutionary time. (I am indebted to the many anonymous artists who have given shape to this creation over the years.) The length of rope one travels between major events (e.g., the formation of galaxies, the birth of the solar system, the emergence of life on earth, photosynthesis — onto more familiar events such as the beginning of agriculture or walking on the moon) is proportional to historical time. Here was an opportunity for me to pull together an awareness of place (cosmically speaking, in this case) with the universal lifeline and journey of creation. Each student carried a candle, lighting it at the birth of the universe into time-space and walking meditatively past smaller candles that designated the major events. They arrived at the last centimeter, where their own lifeline begins, with an enlarged sense of context, story, community, connectedness, and yes, home. Several students mentioned that they wished this had been the first exercise in the course and not the last.

ã ã ã

For my own first assignment in teacher training years ago, I gleefully arrived with Buckminster Fuller's Dymaxion Map. What had appealed to me about this two-dimensional set of triangles — its accuracy, its novelty, and yes, its challenge to the normal spherical representation of the world — was greeted with raised eyebrows and impatient disdain by faculty and students who were "still inside the box." Provocative presentations can still get me into trouble. Luckily, *maps* exist to get me out of trouble — and boxes.

Happy trails!

CHAPTER 2

THE ESSENCE
OF MAPS

If you ask a cartographer about maps, you'll hear about coordinates, meridians, distances, directions, mountains, valleys, water, and the like. But if you look deeper, you'll find surprising complexities, concerns, and questions about things we often take for granted, paralleling my description here about the nature of the *Instructional Map* and its role in helping you navigate the rich, dynamic, and challenging landscape that comprises teaching and learning.

Turnbull and his colleagues (1993), for example, have drawn fascinating connections between maps and Kuhn's (1970, 61) classic work on paradigms in science and research, noting that "there is an important sense in which the map *is* the territory even though paradoxically, the territory is *not* the map." For example, there has long been a very complex dance when new lands are charted, as explorers utilize the best estimates from cartographers to guide their journeys. Columbus found "Indians" in North America because he believed his maps and thought he had arrived in Asia. It wasn't long before the world would conclude otherwise. "Ultimately," Turnbull (1993, 62) continued, "maps and theories gain their power and usefulness from making connections and enabling unanticipated connections."

Kuhn (1970, 109) made the following reference to maps in his discussion of movements within science:

> [Paradigms] provide scientists not only with a map
> but also with some of the directions essential for
> mapmaking. In learning a paradigm, the scientist

acquires theory, methods and standards together, usually in an inextricable mixture.

Teaching, at its simplest, is the delivery of course content. On the *Instructional Map* you can put all of your focus here if you wish. But to maximize student learning, you should recognize the rich mix of variables and interactions comprising the full *Map* —- the intersection of content, context, learner, and yourself; i.e., the meeting of goals, standards, resources, personalities, aptitudes, experiences, motivation, rapport, course design, and delivery.

In *Arctic Dreams,* Barry Lopez (1986, 294) provided some examples of this complexity — of the limits to overly simplified map use even when supported by the most modern of measurement technology and science:

> When the early arctic explorers wrote down in official commentaries what they had seen, they were hesitant to criticize the wisdom of the day, what the esteemed maps indicated. They were prone, in fact, to embellish, in order to make themselves seem more credible. They even believed on occasion that they *had* sensed something where there was nothing because it was ordained that it should happen.

When teachers grade on the curve, for example, do they find the inevitable 16% Ds and Fs because the paradigm they're using requires that percentage? What is lost when this degree of failure is accepted without much question?

Going on, Lopez (1986, 294) painted a complex picture of explorers and their relationship to maps:

> The land, they believed, should corroborate, not contradict, what men knew from sources like Ptolemy about the shape of the world. The accounts of such explorers were read and passed on; the entangled desires and observations of the writers, with a liberal interpretation by cartographers with reputations of their own to protect, perpetuated a geography of hoped-for islands and straits to the west of Europe that could not be substantiated, a geography only of the mind.

When you, as a teacher, *believe* you have done your best to deliver course content in an effective manner, then the responsibility for failure should logically rest with your students. But what of other explanations — for instance, that students might need different exposure to the material, more hands-on experiences, opportunities to practice or apply their learning, images to support the words, or more time or feedback from you? In large introductory classes in particular it can be difficult to provide *everything* that you know would support students' learning.

Some specifics from Lopez (1986, 292) about the difficulties of accurate mapping of the arctic terrain may help clarify this extension of the map metaphor to include *unexplored* terrain and complex issues:

> Fogs and blizzards obscure the reference points important in navigation by topographic map — even compasses can't be consistently relied on here. The closer one gets to the magnetic pole, the stronger the vertical component and the weaker the horizontal component of this electromagnetic field become, causing the needle to wander listlessly, east and west of magnetic north. Corrections for compass declination at certain longitudes and latitudes are useless. Ionospheric disturbances, including magnetic storms and a phenomenon called 'polar cap absorption,' adversely affect radio direction-finding equipment. The frequency of temperature inversions in the summer makes it difficult to align a sextant on an undistorted horizon. And satellite-generated maps showing the extent of the sea ice, sent electronically to ships, are dated in twenty-four hours.

For explorers, the science and art of map reading must coexist. I like to think that the same is true for teachers — that the best instruction is both science and art, coverage and rapport, clarity and mystery, work and joy.

Some new directions in mapping seem promising for explorers and, by extension, perhaps for teachers as well. As Lopez (1986, 295) described it:

> Over the past twenty years, some of the focus of academic geography has shifted away from descriptions of the land and focused instead on landscapes that exist in the human mind. ... The mental maps of both urban dweller and Eskimo may correspond poorly in spatial terms with maps of the same areas

prepared with survey tools and cartographic instruments. But they are proven, accurate guides of the landscape.

While you may follow all of the "rules" about effective delivery, too many of your students may still fail to learn. With the *Instructional Map* I offer you a mechanism for mixing the rules and paradigms about content delivery with ongoing and careful attention to the realities of the student learning landscape.

All of this concern about mapping and paradigms is not to say that orienteering is inherently problematic, but rather to say that every terrain has subtleties that you may be able to discern only through active and attentive involvement. Standing behind your lectern and notes, for example, with preset ideas about content and delivery, may produce mixed results. "Blaming the victim" — the student — won't help. Building rapport and fostering good communication with students will. You'll get ongoing affirmations of what's working as well as feedback about concerns and needed improvements.

The *Instructional Map* is intended to offer you some broad markers about teaching and learning — well-placed lighthouses and buoys, warnings about reefs and shifting sandbars. You, of course, will have to navigate the specific shoals and channels, attentive to weather and water depth, your ship, and your crew.

A Trail Through the Leaves

L ike the *Instructional Map,* Hannah Hinchman's (1997) mix of the visual with the written in *A Trail Through Leaves* adds much to reflection and insight. As an artist, Hinchman has learned to focus on detail, to notice the subtleties of color and shading, and to attend to perspective. When she wants to journal, she uses this artist's focus to create the kind of quiet spaces she needs for important questions to surface. The result is a dynamic and lovely mix of words and images, at times surprising, a source for sorting through all the details and distractions of life and staying on track. I hope the *Instructional Map* can serve a similar function for you in your teaching.

Listen to Hinchman's (1997, 44) call for alertness mixed with spontaneity, only possible with regular attention to the big picture:

> The presence or absence of flow can't be dictated,
> but a person can remain agile and alert, ready to
> recognize and act on whatever comes.

Getting buried in course content can blind you to the need for attending to process, to group dynamics, and even to student learning. In turn, worrying excessively about classroom participation or trying to facilitate a discussion that is bouncing all over the place can distract you from a clear focus on key ideas.

CHAPTER 3

metacognition
AND
metateaching

Metateaching is my own concept, adapted from a number of other concepts. Most important is the notion of *metacognition*, introduced by Meichenbaum et al. (1985) and others to describe the process in which individuals step back and think about their own thinking and learn better how to learn. When I debrief a discovery learning activity, for example, I focus attention on the various ways my students approached a particular problem, what other strategies they might have tried, and what they could do differently next time. I often have them reflect on the *processes* they used to make their decisions, whether or not they gave adequate time for *brainstorming* or *incubating* their ideas, or whether they were trapped by certain rigidities in their thinking — for example, falling prey to a *response set* that prevented them from seeing other possibilities, or to *functional fixedness*, which limited their ideas to traditional applications.

Metateaching can serve a similar function for you, helping you step back from your teaching and develop a working overview of the organizing principles and practices you want to cultivate. It's a way to guide you in your own planning, practice, reflection, and self-awareness. Whenever you approach a teaching assignment, for instance, you can use the *Instructional Map* to think through the range of choices you have: whether to concentrate on facts, on underlying concepts, or on some combination of the two; what emphasis, if any, to put on the emotional (affective) or intuitive aspects of learning; or how to address critical and creative thinking.

The Performer's Skill

In *Teaching and Performing* (1997), I note the many lessons instructors can draw from actors, dancers, singers, and musicians. For example, skilled performers must develop stage awareness and timing, alertness to others on stage, to props and lighting, as well as, to audience reactions — all those subtleties that contribute to the quality of a performance. This awareness, this ability performers develop to watch and hear themselves on stage while they are performing, is akin to metacognition and metateaching.

The Advance Organizer

Other psychological and learning concepts are similar to the notion of metacognition. Introducing the idea of the *advance organizer*, David Ausubel (1963) demonstrated the value of a conceptual preview or framework for helping students organize their thinking and learning. Teachers and texts can help students by laying out the larger underlying concepts and then making periodic references to those concepts as a foundation for all the facts, figures, and ideas that follow.

Let's look at an example. Ralph Smith teaches two large sections of an introductory course in microbiology. While an introductory requirement for some majors, the course serves as an endpoint for others. Students come to the course with a wide assortment of backgrounds and interests. For those with substantial work in chemistry already under their belts, the course includes a review of basic concepts, albeit in a new context and with different examples. For other students, however, it all seems new, complex, and dense with facts and figures.

To accommodate this diversity, Smith utilizes many tools that students value. For example, he makes all of his overheads available on the course web site or as printed handouts. I once facilitated a mid-semester feedback session for this course. During the session, one student told me how helpful it was for her to be able to access these notes and have them in front of her during the lecture itself. While other students raced to keep up with the overheads, this student could instead concentrate on what Smith was saying and augment her notes as needed.

While leading another mid-semester feedback session in another course, this one taught by engineering professor Darrel Fontane, I got direct affirmation from students about the value of an advance organizer for them. When one student recommended that Fontane start each class with a review of previous class material, there was little support for the idea among the other students. Most were eager for new material. As one of the students said: "Hey, I review the material we've covered before each class period. I want to get on to what else I need to know. I don't want to waste my time with the professor on something I can get on my own." Upon hearing this comment, the first student backed off, asking instead for an overview of the new material — a different kind of request that the other students could support.

In my own work with faculty on different campuses, I often find that teachers overestimate the ability of students to integrate masses of new information without an effective preview (advance organizer) or without a periodic return to foundational ideas and principles. Because of their expertise, instructors can be blinded to the needs of many student learners. Paradoxically, having a deep and broad command of course material may prove problematic for some teachers, who might then overlook just how tenuous their students' understanding really is.

Concepts, Rules, and Maps

Identifying the core concepts underlying any content can be critical in helping students understand material at a deep level. That's one reason why concept mapping can be such a powerful tool you can use to help students in their thinking. As you no doubt know, students quickly forget material they "learn" when "cramming" for exams. But their memory for concepts is much more robust. Indeed, concepts can provide a vital scaffolding for more specific bits of information, cues for aiding later recall.

By completing an *Instructional Map* for a particular lesson, you can become more clear about your instructional focus and how best to guide students' learning — and it's all the better if students can learn how to do this for themselves as well.

Jerome Bruner and his associates (e.g., 1967) have contributed much to our understanding of *conceptual learning* — how students conceive ideas and then refine their understanding of those ideas. As a teacher, you can help students understand which *attributes* (or defining qualities) are more critical and how these attributes might *range* (or vary) in value. For example, one attribute that is critical to the concept of teaching — and one that is too often overlooked in our focus on delivery — is student learning. Once we accept learning as an essential and critical attribute for defining effective instruction, we can then ask how much learning (i.e., the range) is needed.

Robert Gagné (e.g., 1985) is widely cited for defining the process by which *discriminations* are organized as *concepts*, which link upward to *rules* and *higher-order rules*. Let's look at an example: the issue of teacher preparation for class. Too little and you are winging it; too much and you may get mired in minutiae and lose sight of the bigger picture. Thus, you learn to *discriminate* between necessary and unnecessary preparation, organizing your experiences into *concepts* (e.g., review, plan, preview) that get linked into *rules* for yourself (e.g., what's the right mix of review, presentation, and preview) and then *higher-order rules* that might factor in responsiveness to student needs as well as your own flexibility.

Novak and Musonda (1991) have gone further in describing the benefits of a *concept map* in which students diagram their understanding. The resulting visual can help students clarify their thinking and literally "see" connections that otherwise exist only as abstractions, relationships memorized. For more visual learners, concept mapping can be an invaluable skill for achieving greater academic success.

For you as a teacher, these concept maps can be a telling look into student thinking, revealing misconceptions, gaps, confusion, and more — insights otherwise gained only through impressions, inferences, and intuition. Asking for these concept maps can also be a wonderful mechanism for nurturing more student-centered (*constructivist*) learning. By taking time to help students learn more about themselves as learners, you open up many new possibilities for independent and cooperative studies.

Jerry Eckert teaches agricultural economics to upper-division and graduate students, and he often uses graphs to illustrate certain principles. Like the concept map, graphs can provide a valuable visual reference to an otherwise abstract, theoretical, or formulaic relationship. In an interview, one of his graduate students told me that he also enjoyed seeing how Eckert developed each graph, what he as the teacher thought about each axis, and how each helped define the variables under study.

But let's look at the concept of "learning" itself and what it could entail. Is it memory? Change in behavior? Change that is permanent or only manifest on a multiple-choice test? Should we include mere *understanding*, or an ability to *apply* new skill or knowledge in other situations? All of these possibilities can be linked to learning through useful lines, arrows, boxes, circles, and such, as demonstrated in the sample map on the following page.

This idea is the essence of the *Instructional Map*.

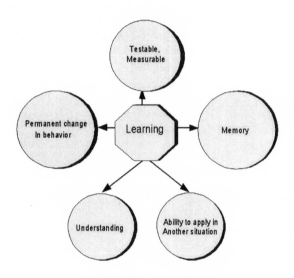

THAT
glorious
vista

Nelson Mandela

How does one survive twenty-seven years in prison and have any heart or spirit left? How can someone experience this degree of extended and brutal oppression from apartheid, but then forgive his oppressors and lead a nation toward a multiracial reconciliation?

Nelson Mandela's story has many lessons for all of us, but one in particular has special meaning for this book. In the very last paragraph of his autobiography, *Long Road to Freedom* (1994, 625), he stops to reflect on his remarkable journey:

> I have walked that long road to freedom. I have tried not to falter; I have made missteps along the way. But I have discovered the secret that after climbing a great hill, one only finds that there are more hills to climb. I have taken a moment here to rest, to steal a view of the glorious vista that surrounds me, to look back on the distance I have come. But I can rest only for a moment, for with freedom come responsibilities, and I dare not linger, for my long walk is not yet ended.

The overview Mandela allows himself is at the heart of my notion of "metateaching." Keeping some perspective is always advisable, especially when spirits lag or confusion reigns. However, perspective can be just as important after the best of classes, giving you an opportunity to slow down and appreciate your own "glorious vista."

centering

Ever felt off balance in your teaching, out of sync with your students, too deep into a discussion or too far afield with a certain digression, especially when there's so much other material you need to cover? In his book, *Journey to Center,* Thomas Crum (1997, 39) offers some ideas I find useful, underscoring a need for us as teachers to stay grounded in the fundamentals of learning:

> Life is change. And change is asking us to color outside the lines. ... Whenever you find yourself in a difficult or stressful situation, returning to a centered state is a good first step. Our usual reactions are to fight, flee or freeze.

Crum then goes on to identify three helpful principles. First *acknowledge:* Be aware, in this case, that you are lost, but avoid self-judgment. It's not inherently good or bad; it just *is.* For teachers, digressions can be trails to greater engagement, the stories that provide intrigue or offer meaning to otherwise dull material — more of what students may see as real.

Second, Crum recommends *acceptance,* taking responsibility for your part in whatever occurs, avoiding blame, and reminding yourself and your students that you are all in this process together. When feelings turn sour after poor performance on an exam, for example, it can be easy to blame students for what they did not learn and avoid the more difficult challenge of reflecting on what you may have failed to teach well enough.

Crum's third principle for centering is to *adapt* — to change and open up to new ideas. When students seem to be shutting down and disengaging from class, and when getting participation feels like pulling teeth, the most natural response may be to speed up, to dance faster. Two colleagues recently described their growing emotional exhaustion when faced with what they perceived to be pervasive student disinterest despite all their efforts to share what they loved about history. As I think about Crum's advice, slowing down to adapt and to find meaningful connections between students and the course material can lead to new insights and responses.

But how, in the moment, can one be centered, aware, more mindful of the bigger picture? On a concrete, physical level Crum makes frequent reference to the power of meditation, to correct breathing, as one way to slow down and retain a clear focus. Another is positive visualization, to stop and "see" yourself teaching as you want — energized, insightful, resourceful, and even inspiring.

CHAPTER 4

THE Instructional Map Explained

Now that we've discussed some of the thinking and philosophy behind the *Instructional Map*, let's examine this tool and its application in greater detail. We begin with an overview of the *Map* and an illustration to give you a sense of what it looks like. We then discuss in depth the three dimensions of the *Map*.

An Overview of the *Instructional Map*

I have developed the diagram that follows for use in a variety of ways — for planning, checking, and reviewing your own instruction or for observing and discussing your instruction with others. The horizontal axis displays the continuum from *teacher-directed* to *student-centered* instruction. The vertical axis extends from *product* to *process*. The continuum from *individual* to *group* learning represents a third dimension, beginning "below" the graph (the word "INDIVIDUAL" is in a smaller font), coming through the center (where you might use small groups), and ending "above" the graph (with the word "GROUP" in a larger font).

On the following pages you will find my most recent version of the *Instructional Map*. The references at the bottom of the map itself and on the second page are from my recent books, *Concepts and Choices for Teaching: Meeting the Challenges in Higher Education* (1996) and *Teaching and Performing: Ideas for Energizing Your Classes* (1997). I believe these concepts and practices reflect many of the more important considerations in effective instruction, and they are

THE INSTRUCTIONAL MAP

Instructor: Date:
Course:
Name:

PROCESS
(thinking, working with abstractions, creating,
communicating, cooperating)

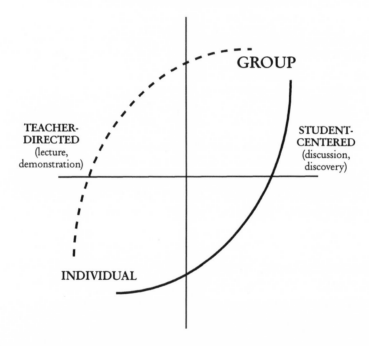

GROUP

**TEACHER-
DIRECTED**
(lecture,
demonstration)

**STUDENT-
CENTERED**
(discussion,
discovery)

INDIVIDUAL

PRODUCT
(knowledge, skills, focusing on the concrete)

CONCEPTS AND CHOICES • teacher knowledge, preparation, experience, and skills • student preparation, motivation, and skills • degree of teacher enthusiasm and student engagement • student participation • meaningfulness of materials and activities • a positive climate • quality of instructional time • quality of feedback

	(low) (high)	*Comments/Notes/* *Plans/Reflections:*
Teacher Knowledge	1 2 3 4 5	
Teacher Preparation/Organization	1 2 3 4 5	
Teacher Enthusiasm/Energy	1 2 3 4 5	
Teacher Clarity	1 2 3 4 5	
Quality of Instructional Time	1 2 3 4 5	
Student Engagement	1 2 3 4 5	
Content/Activity Meaningfulness	1 2 3 4 5	
Positive Learning Climate	1 2 3 4 5	
Feedback to Students	1 2 3 4 5	

If applicable:

Appropriateness of Assessment	1 2 3 4 5
Availability of Practice	1 2 3 4 5
Preview/Review/Closure	1 2 3 4 5

Bloom's Taxonomy

Knowledge	1 2 3 4 5
Comprehension	1 2 3 4 5
Application	1 2 3 4 5
Analysis	1 2 3 4 5
Synthesis	1 2 3 4 5
Evaluation	1 2 3 4 5

Overall Course/ Presentation Challenge	1 2 3 4 5

Additional notes, etc.:

intended to be cues and reminders for you when you plan, check, or reflect upon your teaching. You can use the blank spaces provided for notes, ideas, questions, and the like.

The First Continuum: Teacher-directed to Student-centered

The horizontal axis on the *Instructional Map* is dedicated to approaches that can be arrayed between a strictly *teacher-directed* format and one that is essentially *student-centered*. When you think about particular content and a certain group of students, how do you decide among a lecture presentation, a class discussion, some combination of the two, an in-class writing assignment, or a small-group activity? There are times when you may want to start with a formal presentation and then move into a discussion that taps into student interests. Indeed, there are myriad possibilities and combinations along this continuum.

Although you can cover a great deal of material efficiently in a lecture, you may miss opportunities for nurturing deeper learning if you restrict yourself to that one approach. On the other hand, while discussions can be lively and highly engaging, they can miss important points and key concepts. Everyone, yourself included, can get energized by the exchange or dragged down by mass inertia or resistance. Even when good points are made, the domination of a few students may discourage others from participating.

Denny Phillips is a very energetic teacher who regularly treats his Speech/Communication classes to a real show as he moves from lecture to video or audio clip and back again to lecture. However, he is also attentive to the need to get his students involved, and so he routinely asks questions. While some are rhetorical and only serve to set up his next comments, other questions are intended to provoke reaction, discussion, and reflection. Often after such a question, Phillips will wait for a response, allowing students a few seconds to think about what they want to say. After filling so much of the classroom space with his own enthusiastic presence, the resulting silence during these "wait times" can be deafening. However, these spaces serve an important purpose for the class, marking a shift for Phillips from a *teacher-directed* mode to one that is more *student-centered*.

To help you think more about your choices along this continuum, consider the following questions:

- Who should learn what and when?
- Are there some students who require more than a lecture presentation, or more than a discussion?
- How much is lost when students are passive, or when they have little opportunity in class to work with the course content? How much will they recall later? Will it suffice to relegate more active student involvement to labs, recitation sessions, or various electronic discussions — e-mail, listservs, chat rooms, and the like?
- To deepen learning, when could students be active, and for how long?
- What amount of lecture material is covered in course readings? What could be summarized on handouts or placed on the course web site?

The Second Continuum: Product to Process

The vertical axis on the *Instructional Map* gets you thinking about *product* and *process* — the time and effort you want to give to the learning of facts or skills versus the time you want to dedicate to critical and creative thinking, decision making and problem solving, teamwork, cooperation, or conflict resolution. For example, when you base grades solely on student responses to knowledge-based, objective examinations, you may skew course emphasis toward *product* (knowledge, skills). When you require students to write essays, on the other hand, your grading necessarily becomes more subjective and more reflective of what I refer to as *process* skills (thinking, creating).

Working along this continuum can help you develop a better blend of objectives, ranging, for example, from the lowest levels on Bloom's (1956) cognitive hierarchy — from knowledge to comprehension and application — to the highest — from analysis to synthesis and evaluation. Whether you're planning lecture content, considering questions for discussion, or writing examination questions, you can always get a mix of the various levels represented by this taxonomy, a range from surface (e.g., recall) to deeper learning (e.g., problem solving and creativity).

One very complex issue here is the degree of objectivity you want in your course. Many students, especially those who are younger and less mature, are quite used to a focus on information, facts, set procedures, formulas, and the like — what they can memorize, practice, and repeat back on exams. By the time they make it into higher education, these students may have become quite good at "psyching out" what their teachers want and what their texts require. Asking for something different from students — what may be beyond mere repetition — can frustrate many of them. Our challenge as teachers, however, may be to "stay the course," to convey empathy, and to help students reframe that frustration as a potential catalyst for deeper learning and growth. We function like "cognitive midwives" for the mind.

For anesthesiologists Pete Hellyer and Jamie Gaynor at Colorado State University's Veterinary Teaching Hospital, attempts to do more with problem-based learning illustrate some key issues on this product-process continuum. When I asked second-year students there for their reactions to a whole-class analysis of a particular case, I got very clear messages about the balance needed between knowledge and analysis. A problem-based session can be very engaging, they said, but only if they had enough of a knowledge base to be able to participate productively. Otherwise, they'd be lost and frustrated. Giving information in class has its place, but only to a point. Then these students wanted to try to use the time available in a more challenging and interactive manner, to think through cases, much like they will encounter once they're finished with their schooling.

Looking at this process within a developmental framework, Perry (1981) noted how students tend to arrive at college thinking very dualistically, about answers that are "right" or "wrong" Their reference ("agency") for truth is external, typically the teacher or the text. As they mature as independent thinkers, however, students become more comfortable with accepting a variety of opinions — what Perry terms "multiplicity." Once students have opened up to other ways of thinking, they can then begin to evaluate those perspectives and whether any have coherent sources of support — what Perry terms "relativism." Finally, with additional intellectual maturation, students become better able to consider various viewpoints. They then either modify or confirm their own thinking, moving to what Perry terms "committed relativism."

As a teacher, your role in facilitating growth along Perry's developmental hierarchy can mean that you push students out of their preferred comfort with objective bits of memorizable information and into the real world of complex interrelationships and subjective judgments. Consciously moving between product and process can help students link basic knowledge with underlying concepts and principles.

You can also think of this continuum as stretching from the concrete to the abstract, from facts to theories. On one end is everything you can see and touch, organize and manipulate; on the other end are ideas, those mental constructs we create to interconnect and explain what we experience more directly.

To help you think more about your choices along the product-process continuum, consider the following questions:

- What are your goals? Do you want a mix of objectives as defined by Bloom's hierarchy?
- Do you want to promote deeper learning — to have students apply their knowledge, skills, and understanding; to practice solving problems or think more about the complexities of the real world?
- Do you feel pressured by students to cover only what is on the test?
- Do you avoid more attention to critical and creative thinking because of the inherent subjectivity in evaluating them?
- To deepen learning, should your students be active? For how long?
- What amount of lecture material could you cover through course readings or through some other mechanism?

The Third Continuum: Individual Learning to Group Learning

Individual assignments, both in and out of class, can help students learn actively and independently. Small-group work can provide opportunities for students to use what they're learning, to get involved in team projects, and to receive more immediate support, assistance, and feedback from their classmates. Large groups can let you move quickly through a lot of material when you lecture, integrate the latest findings, field questions, clarify what may be confusing, and offer alternative examples or explanations.

While David and Roger Johnson (1994) argue convincingly for the value of cooperative learning activities, individual account-ability and direct, whole-class instruction will undoubtedly con-tinue as viable instructional options. Historically, lectures predate the printing presses but have endured because of their efficiency and flexibility. Discussion sections have long provided opportunities for more active exchanges in smaller group settings. Readings and assignments detail what each individual student has to do. More recently, teachers in higher education have begun to explore alter-natives to this traditional mix of course design and delivery. Some are using cases to organize whole-class discussions, even in large lecture halls. Some are stopping periodically to allow students to discuss a question with classmates nearby, probing understanding before moving on. Others will structure cooperative learning activi-ties into course requirements and turn over some class time for students to make presentations on various topics.

Using the *Instructional Map* can allow you to periodically check this continuum, reminding yourself of alternative possibilities for organizing your instruction.

For example, artist Nanci Erskine regularly mixes several in-structional approaches in her studio courses on drawing. She'll often begin class with an introduction, a presentation on a particular idea, and an overview of the assignment for that day. Students then spend the remainder of the class period working on their drawings. What then brings small groups into play is the positive and supportive climate Erskine works to foster in class. She encourages students to give each other support and assistance, feedback and encourage-ment, different perspectives and ideas. It's a very dynamic process in which students move in and out of interactions with classmates as they need help or are asked for help — in short, a fluid and self-organizing community.

Listening
AND
Hearing

bell hooks

In *Wounds of Passion*, bell hooks draws on her experiences as one of the few African American students at Stanford in the 1960s to describe her own journey as a writer. Author of sixteen books since then, many on the intersection of ethnicity and gender in American society, she details the isolation she felt in her college classrooms when she tried to speak about these issues.

Listen to the following and think about what you, as a teacher, can do to focus more on process and student experiences when these kinds of deep divisions emerge, and when the traditional format leaves some students on the margins (1997, 98-99):

> When I speak everyone stops to listen but then no one hears. They are all white and they are all here to celebrate being female. They do not want to hear that the shared reality of femaleness does not mean an equal share of powerlessness. There are no southern white girls. If there are, they remain silent. For no one who grows up in the apartheid south believes that the lot of black women and white women is the same, not even those who share the same class. Race makes the difference. And it is enough of a difference to preclude the possibility of common expression.

> They listen to me but they don't hear. They don't have to hear. This is what it means to be among the colonizers; you do not have to listen to what the colonized have to say, especially if their ideas come from experience and not from books. They ask you if there is a book they can read that will explain what

you are talking about. I can hear everything the white girls who are my roommates and my peers are saying about the condition of women, can read my tattered copy of Simone de Beauvoir and be down with the discussion. When it comes to thinking about the intersection of race and gender, I stand alone.

THE
perils of
Banking

Paulo Freire

Among educators in this century, none stands taller than Brazilian Paulo Freire, champion of the "oppressed" and godfather of literacy campaigns worldwide, offering hope and possibility where only stagnation and despair had existed before.

Listen to his classic critique of traditional schooling as a "banking notion," registering deposits of information but neglecting critical and creative thinking. Think about the range of options embodied in the *Instructional Map* — the attention to process skills and to active student learning (Freire 1970, 57):

> It follows logically from the banking notion of consciousness that the educator's role is to regulate the way the world "enters into" the students. The teacher's task is to organize a process which already occurs spontaneously, to "fill" the students by making deposits of information which he or she considers to constitute true knowledge. And since people "receive" the world as passive entities, education should make them more passive still, and adapt them to the world. The educated individual is the adapted person, because she or he is better "fit" for the world. Translated into practice, this concept is well suited for the purposes of the oppressors, whose tranquility rests on how well people fit the world the oppressors have created, and how little they question it.

> The more completely the majority adapt to the purposes which the dominant minority prescribe for

them (thereby depriving them of the right to their own purposes), the more easily the minority can continue to prescribe. The theory and practice of banking education serves this end efficiently. Verbalistic lessons, reading requirements, the methods for evaluating "knowledge," the distance between the teacher and the taught, the criteria for promotion: everything in this ready-to-wear approach seems to obviate thinking.

flow

Mihaly Csikszentmihalyi's book, *Flow*, is a clear call for risk taking, for stretching our talents and affirming our gifts in the cauldron of challenge. Getting to the top end of Maslow's hierarchy, that possibility for "self-actualization," is not something that happens magically. It requires effort, focus, and perseverance. In the nature-nurture debate about whether great teachers are born or made, Csikszentmihalyi would come down strongly on the "nurture" side of education and energy investment. Our students would benefit from that same investment.

When we're lost or confused, our spirits can slip. When our actions are aligned with our goals and values, we can soar (1990, 37-39):

> Whenever information disrupts consciousness by threatening its goals, we have a condition of inner disorder, or *psychic entropy*, a disorganization of the self that impairs its effectiveness. ...

> The opposite state from the condition of psychic entropy is optimal experience. When the information that keeps coming into awareness is congruent with goals, psychic energy flows effortlessly.

The *Instructional Map* can help you stay grounded in your core beliefs about teaching and learning.

Alignment of actions, beliefs, and values makes sense. But beyond that is your own energy and enthusiasm for teaching. People are happiest, insists Csikszentmihalyi (1990, 99), when they are involved in activities that "demand a relatively high investment of psychic energy." Intriguingly, Csikszentmihalyi goes on to extend this line of reasoning even further, noting that one's enjoyment

47

(your enjoyment as a teacher, for example) "does not depend on *what* you do, but rather on *how* you do it." As a teacher, the excitement you have about your subject must translate into an engaging process with students. Otherwise, the "flow" — and everyone's energy — will be dammed.

For example, what is lost when your instruction is dull, routine, unimaginative (1990, 112)?

> Even when children are taught music, the usual problem often arises: too much emphasis is placed on how they perform, and too little on what they experience.

Just as you need to find flow in your teaching, so will students do best when they are also flowing, stretched, challenged, and engaged at optimal levels.

Optimal experience is not just about activity, however. It's not just in what we do as teachers. Flow in learning requires the active and focused involvement of students as well. For example, even in lecture or during the silences within classroom discussions, there are rich opportunities for stretching and learning (1990, 110-111):

> As the Yaqui sorcerer taught the anthropologist Carlos Castaneda, even the intervals of silence between sounds, if listened to closely, can be exhilarating. ...

> As one develops analytic listening skills, the opportunities to enjoy music increase geometrically.

Csikszentmihalyi (1990, 119) then goes on to describe the state of affairs when we lose our focus, when students just drift:

> Contrary to what we tend to assume, the normal state of the mind is chaos. ... When we are left alone, with no demands on attention, the basic disorder of the mind reveals itself. With nothing to do, it begins to follow random patterns, usually stopping to consider something painful or disturbing. Unless a person knows how to give order to his or her thoughts, attention will be attracted to whatever is most problematic at the moment. ... Entropy is the normal state of consciousness — a condition that is neither useful nor enjoyable.

CHAPTER 5

using
THE
Instructional Map

I use the *Instructional Map* for a visual, conceptual, and pragmatic preview before class, a quick check on what I have planned, and the various activities and transitions that will be necessary. It's the *gestalt* I want, a reminder of the big picture, the overview — what I term *metateaching*. I'm regularly reminded of all the intersections inherent in the teaching and learning processes, the mix of content and classroom with student variables (e.g., background, interests, preparation, abilities, values, skills) and my own qualities (e.g., skills, sensitivities, interests, values, energy).

After completing my notes for class and thinking through my goals and what I want students to learn, I then sketch out a map and locate the central activities in the order I want. Mapping the process in this way helps me step back from all the details and complexities of the content and ensures that I give adequate time and attention to key concepts — the ideas underlying the course that students will remember long after forgetting the details. Whether *you* use it for planning, for observing, or as a reference for yourself during instruction or afterward, the *Instructional Map* can give you useful cues or reminders about factors that have longstanding impact on students' learning.

In this chapter, I will discuss the meaning of the terms or phrases that appear on the *Instructional Map*. Read this chapter before using the Map. Familiarize yourself with the factors listed. However, please view the *Map* as a dynamic instrument. In other words, it should suit your own purposes. So feel free to add other factors that might be important to you in the context in which you work.

You may also find it useful to let students in on this process. Show them the *Map* and explain what you are trying to improve upon, along with what feedback you are seeking from them. Periodically, you could ask the students to give you their reactions, either verbally or in writing. This can be a valuable addition to mid-semester or end-of-semester evaluations, giving you clear indications of what works and signs of what does not. Be sure to press students about their concerns, and ask for recommendations for improvement. Addressing concerns directly in this manner provides a double benefit: it improves the course and boosts student morale at the same time.

If you invite peers in to observe your teaching, ask them to read this chapter as well so that they are familiar with the factors upon which you'd like to focus. Again, you can tailor the *Map* to better accommodate your needs, modifying some factors, eliminating others, and adding a few new ones. As with *constructivist learning* and students, there are real advantages when you become more active in defining qualities that are important to your own teaching. These qualities then become more *real* — and more meaningful to you on a personal basis.

The *Instructional Map's* Terms and Phrases

When should your instruction become more student-centered so that students can have some practice with the skills, information, and ideas you are presenting? When should you rethink the conceptual level of your material, how much you intend to pitch at a knowledge or skill (product) level, and how much you can pitch at a deeper, conceptual (process) level? When could you vary your plans for the whole class and focus instruction on individuals or small groups?

The references on the *Instructional Map* can help cue you about factors long identified with effective instruction. A brief explanation of each term or phrase follows.

Teacher Knowledge, Preparation, and Organization

What do you need to do before you present a particular lesson? How will you conceptualize your role in content delivery? For example, Sharon Anderson often agonizes about the degree to which

NOTE: You can use this front page as a visual reference for planning, observing, or assessing your instruction. You can write your own notes in the space provided about what occurred, what could have happened, what you might do, and so on. At the bottom of the page are selected conceptual references to cue your thinking.

Instructor/Course: Date:
Teacher Goals:

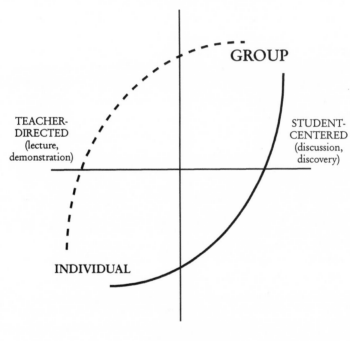

CONCEPTS AND CHOICES • teacher knowledge and skills • student preparation, motivation, and skills • degree of teacher enthusiasm and student engagement • student participation • meaningful material and activities • a positive climate • quality of instructional time • quality of feedback

	(low)	(high)	Comments/Notes/ Plans/Reflections:
Teacher Knowledge	1 2 3 4 5		
Teacher Preparation/Organization	1 2 3 4 5		
Teacher Enthusiasm/Energy	1 2 3 4 5		
Teacher Clarity	1 2 3 4 5		
Quality of Instructional Time	1 2 3 4 5		
Student Engagement	1 2 3 4 5		
Content/Activity Meaningfulness	1 2 3 4 5		
Positive Learning Climate	1 2 3 4 5		
Feedback to Students	1 2 3 4 5		

If applicable:

Appropriateness of Assessment	1 2 3 4 5
Availability of Practice	1 2 3 4 5
Preview/Review/Closure	1 2 3 4 5

Bloom's Taxonomy

Knowledge	1 2 3 4 5
Comprehension	1 2 3 4 5
Application	1 2 3 4 5
Analysis	1 2 3 4 5
Synthesis	1 2 3 4 5
Evaluation	1 2 3 4 5

Overall Course/ Presentation Challenge	1 2 3 4 5

Additional notes, etc.:

she is willing to take the lead in particular classes. As she works with graduate students in a school counseling program, she wants to facilitate their own discovery of critical issues as much as possible. She strive to minimize her intrusiveness into a process that she believes must be primarily student-centered. She wants to model a "client-centered" approach whenever possible. Yet, she still must be the expert leading a group of novices. What is the right balance of facilitation and direct instruction?

Student Knowledge, Preparation, and Motivation

What will your students need to be successful? Teachers complain about this concept in all levels of education. Some students may come unprepared and make participation difficult; they may need extensive remedial help, or they may ask questions about material you've already covered. Other students may feel peer pressure to remain quiet, playing the "slacker" role. Some may have enrolled in more courses than they can handle. Far too many students seem doomed to be forever stretched, pulled between too many credits, work demands, the allurements of the collegiate social scene, and their own limitations in managing new freedoms and responsibilities.

In my own courses, I often feel pulled in a variety of directions: empathetic toward those students who need to work long hours to pay for college, but cognizant of my responsibilities to safeguard the standards of the course; understanding when students decide to take on a lot of courses during a particular semester but leery about the effects this will have on the requirements for my own course; aware of the importance of using class time to respond to student questions but hesitant to repeat what students should learn through study outside of class.

Teacher Enthusiasm and Student Engagement

Ken Klopfenstein (Mathematics) faces a real dilemma when he lectures. He loves the material, and his students appreciate his skill and energy as a teacher. However, he's doing all the work in class, or most of it anyway. Sure, students take notes. But in general they are not much more active than that, except for the occasional question. And even that is problematic, because Ken's experience and skill in lecturing — his clarity, appropriate pacing, use of rhetorical questions, pauses and examples, and sensitivity to student reactions — are such that students rarely raise substantive questions. He's that good.

So what's the problem? Ken finds his own energies waning when students sink into a comfortable passivity. He's not getting much back from them, no real interaction. There's nothing dynamic about the lecture process. It's more of a one-way flow of explanation. Not surprisingly, he has come to value what happens within a cooperative learning structure — the active participation required of students, the energy they have to invest, and the frustrations that inevitably occur when they have to take more of the lead while learning new material. Of course, it's easier for them to sit back and let him do the work. Isn't that what they paid their tuition for?

Klopfenstein must, then, walk this tightrope, providing enough energetic leadership to keep the class moving through a demanding curriculum while insisting on the active involvement of students in cooperative groups, where their engagement is high although they are frustrated and uncomfortable at times.

Student Participation

What do you notice about students who are involved and those who aren't? Can you assume that students who are not participating have checked out intellectually?

I've been surprised on several occasions when I perceive a level of disengagement and later find out from students that they were actually having a very rich and active internal response. In one particular literature course, several students told me of their appreciation when their instructor, Gil Findlay, honored their desire to stay quiet and let their reflections remain personal. Barbara, a young African American student from Denver, insisted that this was her favorite course because the biographical reading materials were so rich in personal meaning for her. "I hear that," I said, "but you looked disengaged. You didn't join in the discussion or volunteer any response when Findlay solicited reactions." "No," she said, "I was thinking, and I appreciate that he lets me stay quiet." Findlay's use of written journal reactions provides everyone with a more private vehicle for communicating their reflections to him.

The point is that student participation can be a very private matter, and we may trivialize its impact on learning if we look only for the more public response in class. Being alert to participation can help you better explore its role, from the public to the private.

Meaningful Materials and Activities

Do the content and activities of your course seem meaningful? How can you tell? What would make for greater meaning? We know from much research on learning that students will remember more of what is relevant to them, what connects to their deeper interests and values. When students think they are just jumping hurdles, doing what they need to do to get the grade and move on, and when they don't see the relevance or meaning of the material, then their motivation and recall both suffer.

Can you connect your material to something in the news or to some other compelling issue? Among your students, who cares and why is the material important to them? What's really at stake? "Can these stakes be raised," as they ask in the theatre? And once students are hooked, can you keep them connected with periodic references to these deeper issues?

Sandy Kern (Physics) will use common examples to help students understand the fundamentals of physics. He has to be on his toes because there are many times when his first example doesn't get the idea across completely or when a student's question masks a real confusion about some principle. With a ball, for example, Kern can demonstrate something about acceleration, velocity, the effects of gravity, or the brilliance of a pitcher like Greg Maddux!

Nat Kees (Education) taught a course on wellness in which her own benchmark for success was more about the impact of wellness on the lives of her students and less about their mastery of course content as reflected in exam performance. Accordingly, she used a great deal of reflective listening, acceptance, and empathy in class as part of a student-centered focus intended to facilitate a deep connection between the course material and the lives of the students. Issues about stress and balance that emerged from the readings, videotapes, and presentations by guest speakers were routinely held up as mirrors students could use to reflect upon their own lives. Even the choice of course readings was left up to each student so that learning could be more personally meaningful.

A Positive Climate

Is the overall climate of your course positive, both in and outside of class? What might make it better? We now know a great deal about the relationship between student morale and learning — what factors promote engagement and risk taking, for example. It can take time to build a sense of community in your class, but the quality and depth of learning that results invariably makes this a good investment. If students feel respected by you and their classmates, and if they can feel safe, they may be better able to admit to what they don't know or what they're confused about before you move on to new material. They may even feel safe enough to debate you or their classmates, even if they hold a minority viewpoint.

We know from the work of various developmentalists — Piaget, Kohlberg, Gilligan, Perry — or those who work with critical thinking and values that finding the wherewithal to question any source of external authority, to ask for coherent documentation and, ultimately, to decide for oneself ought to be a fundamental goal of education at the postsecondary level.

Nanci Erskine (Art) is very conscious of creating the kind of climate that encourages students to explore different media so that they can offer constructive feedback and direction. Nanci wants to see students reach within themselves to find their own sources of creativity. She worries about teachers who essentially clone themselves, even if they do so in an unconscious way. Thus, she is consciously "non-intrusive" in her feedback and comments on student work. She usually listens first to hear the student's self-appraisal. She'll then offer feedback or guidance, but only in a personal or self-referenced form — "I think ..." or "I believe ..." or "It seems to me that ..." or "I like this because ... ."

Quality of Instructional Time

Do you use your class time well? What do you lose when class starts late or when students start preparing to leave before class is officially over? Is the quality of your time together high? Are students engaged at a deep level, or are they simply busy writing down what will later appear on an exam? Are students having success? Are they learning? If you can refer to these questions as concentric circles — with allotted time as the outer circle subsuming instructional time, engaged time, and student learning — you may find a useful framework for rethinking your classes.

Sandy Kern (Physics) will frequently pose a question to the 300 students in his introductory course for non-majors. He then gives students a few minutes to discuss their ideas with their neighbors. Then he'll poll the class to see how many students came up with what answers. While this process takes some time, it proves very valuable for Kern as a check for understanding before moving on. If there is too much confusion, he'll shift gears, find other examples, and reteach a particular idea. Why move on if too many students have missed something essential? Especially in disciplines that build upon knowledge in a sequential manner, gaps in understanding can prove increasingly fatal as the semester proceeds.

Feedback to Students

Research evidence clearly shows that students benefit enormously from instructor feedback. When students can monitor their own progress, they can make better adjustments in their learning — they can rethink misconceptions, clarify what you really want, and break their learning tasks down into more manageable chunks.

By using a small-group format in class for some discussions and assignments, Irene Vernon (English) is able to visit with each group, listen in, and then offer feedback to individuals or the group as a whole. Gil Findlay (English), as mentioned earlier, uses a journal requirement to offer his feedback in a way that allows for more personal and confidential exchanges. Nanci Erskine (Art) schedules fifteen or twenty minutes with each student in her studio drawing class, both around mid-semester and at the end of the semester, to have them spread out their work for feedback. For Nanci, it is important that these critiques be constructive so that students receive useful ideas for improvement.

Appropriateness of Assessment

Understandably, students are very concerned about grading policies and practices. So the clarity of your expectations becomes critical. For example, Bill Wright (Biology) will offer a review session just before an exam to address any questions or confusions and to clarify what he expects students to know and understand. Indeed, Wright insists that he often does his best teaching during these sessions. He'll start in the early evening, usually around 7 p.m., but he promises to stay until there are no more questions (sometimes the sessions go past midnight!). What makes the teaching so rich for him is that students come motivated, with questions in mind. They are focused and prepared to really engage with the material, often going way beyond the factual knowledge base into applications and speculations.

Availability of Practice

Many students seem to get lost because they don't really work with the ideas under study. They hear the professor's explanation in class and read their texts, but their recall invariably suffers when they cannot apply the learning in some context. In a mid-level microbiology course, Ralph Smith and Erica Suchman have been exploring the benefits of a poster project on diseases that teams of students must complete. What impressed me when I debriefed their classes at mid-semester was the students' appreciation for the opportunity to apply their learning in a new and creative way, even though most groups experienced real frustration in finding times to meet outside of class.

Preview, Review, Closure, and Recall

A longstanding bit of advice for instructors is to tell students where you're going in a particular lesson, take them there, and then tell them where you've taken them. As is true for the *Instructional Map* generally, sharing with students an overview of the central concepts under study and then reminding them of those ideas throughout the lesson can prove very valuable as students try to make sense of all the information they're getting. When I debriefed students at mid-semester in Darrel Fontane's engineering class, they were nearly unanimous in their appreciation for his providing a preview (advance organizer), although most were opposed to taking any class time to review material they could learn on their own. During a mid-semester debriefing for Kenton Bird (Technical Journalism), students were very appreciative of his use of multimedia (videotapes and audiotapes) to illustrate certain concepts.

Bloom's Taxonomy

Making use of Bloom's taxonomy — knowledge, understanding, application, analysis, synthesis, and evaluation — can help you get the kind of distribution of questions and focus you want in your courses — a mix of information and thinking. For example, students in second-year anesthesiology courses were very clear when they explained to me that while they enjoyed a problem-based approach in class, they also recognized their need for a certain knowledge base before they could meaningfully join in the case analysis.

A Tool with Wide Application

I encourage you to experiment with the *Instructional Map*, noting the impact of various decisions on your teaching, your students, their learning, and your courses.

By writing in the mix of activities for any given class, you can plan for the way you want them to combine in meeting your goals and objectives. By referencing your map during class, you can get quick reminders at any particular time of what more you want to accomplish, thus helping yourself stay on track. By reviewing the map after class, you can reflect on the implications of what really did happen. By sharing your map with a colleague who comes to observe, you can have a useful reference for feedback and discussion. And by taking the map with you when you observe someone else teach or when you team teach, you have a handy reference for discussing your work together.

THE
Artist's
Way

Julia Cameron's *The Artist's Way* has proven very popular for people who want help in getting unblocked. The book is a treatise on creativity and the personal understanding, courage, and initiative you need to contribute more that is original and yours.

As a successful screenwriter, Cameron has much to offer teachers, who must not only create connections among varied sources of knowledge, old and new, but also find ways to present their ideas in clear and engaging ways to audiences of students who come with widely varying backgrounds, preparation, and motivations. Cameron's references to direction and map are mostly about self-awareness, but what better place to begin than on the *Map* of yourself — who you are and what you believe and what you want from students. Every decision about teaching — even the decision to have an inclusive classroom discussion — must start with you.

For Cameron, it all begins with self-awareness (1992, 81):

> The process of identifying a self inevitably involves loss as well as gain. We discover our boundaries ... we lose our misconceptions. As we eliminate ambiguity, we lose illusion as well. We arrive at clarity, and clarity creates change.

As we understand more about these internal boundaries, we become better able to navigate those boundaries in our teaching — boundaries between what we do and what we want students to learn, between knowledge and thinking, between individual initiative and group dynamics.

Artists in all walks of life learn to go within, Cameron notes (1992, 92):

> By listening to the creator within, we are led to our right path. On that path, we find friends, lovers,

money and meaningful work. Very often, when we cannot seem to find an adequate supply, it is because we are insisting on a particular human source of supply. We must learn to let the flow manifest itself where it will — not where we will it.

Knowing more about the broad picture of teaching, the big concepts as described in the *Instructional Map*, can help you use more of your intuition about timing, pace, direction — all those subtle factors that can mean so much for sustaining student engagement and learning.

observations, presentations, AND student Reflections

Using the *Instructional Map* to Get Feedback on Your Teaching

While it was initially designed to help teachers plan, conduct, and reflect upon their own teaching, the *Instructional Map* has also proven useful as a mechanism for guiding feedback from observers. When watching a colleague teach I may get so focused on the content that I lose sight of other factors that are tied to learning: student engagement; the climate in class; the opportunity to practice; and the teacher's preparation, organization, clarity, and enthusiasm. Having the following versions of the *Instructional Map* for notes and comments has been useful as a reminder of all these variables.

I tend to use the space on the front of the *Map* for general notes and for my perceptions about:

- what seemed primarily informational and what called for more critical and creative thinking,
- what seemed more teacher-directed and what seemed more student-centered,
- where there might have been more group focus, or
- where a question asked by a student could have been thrown back for the entire class to consider.

I also use the *Map* to indicate the order of events — what happened first, second, and so on — using numbers and approximate times as reference points to class chronology. This helps later when

Observer Feedback about Instruction

Instructor/Course: Date:

Teacher Goals:

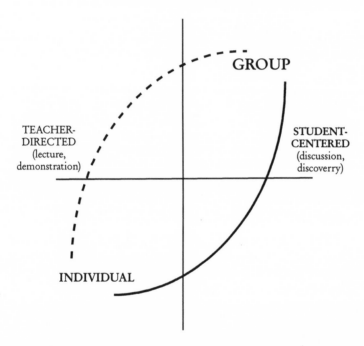

PROCESS
(thinking, working with abstractions, creating, communicating, cooperating)

GROUP

TEACHER-DIRECTED
(lecture, demonstration)

STUDENT-CENTERED
(discussion, discovery)

INDIVIDUAL

PRODUCT
(knowledge, skills, focusing on the concrete)

CONCEPTS AND CHOICES • teacher knowledge, preparation, and skill • student preparation, motivation, and skills • degree of teacher enthusiasm and student engagement • student participation • meaningfulness of materials and activities • a positive climate • quality of instructional time • quality of feedback

---

	(low) (high)	Comments/Notes/ Plans/Reflections:
Teacher Knowledge	1 2 3 4 5	
Teacher Preparation/Organization	1 2 3 4 5	
Teacher Enthusiasm/Energy	1 2 3 4 5	
Teacher Clarity	1 2 3 4 5	
Quality of Instructional Time	1 2 3 4 5	
Student Engagement	1 2 3 4 5	
Content/Activity Meaningfulness	1 2 3 4 5	
Positive Learning Climate	1 2 3 4 5	
Feedback to Students	1 2 3 4 5	

If applicable:

Appropriateness of Assessment	1 2 3 4 5
Availability of Practice	1 2 3 4 5
Preview/Review/Closure	1 2 3 4 5

Bloom's Taxonomy

Knowledge	1 2 3 4 5
Comprehension	1 2 3 4 5
Application	1 2 3 4 5
Analysis	1 2 3 4 5
Synthesis	1 2 3 4 5
Evaluation	1 2 3 4 5

Overall Course/ Presentation Challenge	1 2 3 4 5

Additional notes, etc.:

I want to talk to the teacher about the class. It provides a convenient reference and cues for remembering the details. It's not just my feedback that is the focus here; I also want to share what I noticed so that the teacher and I can have something tangible to discuss, a starting point for conversation about improvements and possibilities.

I'll also use any available space, including the margins, for other notes — for example, about pacing and the use of class time, or my perception of classroom climate and what seemed to be helping students focus and learn. I'll avoid using negative signs (-) and instead use question marks (?) when I have a concern or an idea. I'll use positive (+) signs when I think something was effective.

On the second page of the *Instructional Map*, I'll use the qualities listed on the left side as observer references during the lesson, and then for summary assessments at the end if appropriate. In the space on the right, I'll make my notes and questions about what I think is working — e.g., "effective vocal projection, occasional humor, appropriate pacing with periodic pauses and checks for reactions, relaxed but focused classroom climate, responsive to questions."

I'll also add ideas I have as suggestions for improvement. For example, I might think that a video clip about a particular case would add something of value, or that calling students by name would spark more engagement. I also may record certain frequencies, like the number of times the teacher will check for understanding (e.g., "Everyone OK with that?"), launch quickly into a response to a question, or check first to see if everyone has heard adequately.

When you're working with other teachers, the *Instructional Map* can serve as a stimulus for planning, analysis, feedback, and exploratory discussions. Before coming into class, I can use it as a reference for discussions with teachers about the exact focus of my observations — what they want me to look for. I always try to ask for foci that I can quantify — for example, which students participate in discussion, who asks what kinds of questions, or the "wait time" the teacher provides after asking a question. When the teacher and I can talk again after class, I'll begin with my observations, then discuss what the teacher wanted me to look for, and finally share any other thoughts I may have. While one-time observations are useful, however, I cannot stress enough the benefits of repeated visits — how important it is to get to know teachers, to break through that isolation we all face, to share ideas and explore possibilities, to talk to some of the students and get a feel for the class as a whole, and to be able to follow up on earlier conversations.

Using *the Instructional Map* to Offer Feedback on Student Presentations

Another way you can use the *Instructional Map* is to give students feedback on their presentations. In what follows, note that all I've really done is replace the word "teacher" with the word "presenter." You can apply the same qualities that underlie effective instruction to student presentations; they can be held to the same criteria. Indeed, combining the excitement that inevitably surrounds a public performance with student awareness of the importance of factors like knowledge, preparation, organization, and clarity can help many students improve the quality of their presentations.

When I give copies of this form out to students in my own courses, I take a few minutes to explain the various terms and what I think will be most useful in terms of feedback — i.e., providing details about what worked, what didn't, and why and avoiding more general assessments like "good" and "bad." Again, by using these ideas, students can develop a greater awareness of and sophistication about their own learning processes.

Using the *Instructional Map* to Help Students Reflect on Learning and Instruction

Another use of the *Instructional Map* is as a "Learning Map." With the alterations that follow, you can give students a mechanism for thinking about their own learning, what their role is in the instructional process beyond simplistic "consumerism," and how their skills, attitudes, and preparation fit with your expectations and expertise. Learning is fundamentally a shared endeavor, a path teachers and students must walk together. Real empowerment here means that, like their instructors, students must "show up" intellectually and emotionally.

Exposing students to these ideas in the Learning Map will also equip them to give you more of the feedback you need about their progress, successes, and concerns. What are you doing that is working, and what is proving to be problematic? With some common understanding, you can have a running conversation with your students — one that benefits you and your students.

FEEDBACK
ABOUT STUDENT PRESENTATIONS

Group/Presenter: Date:

Lesson Goals:

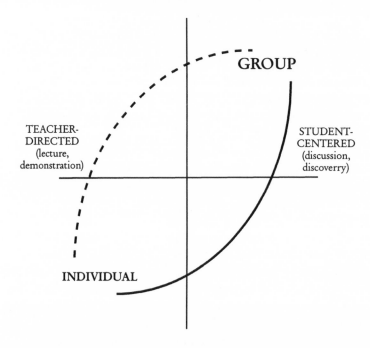

PROCESS
(thinking, working with abstractions, creating,
communicating, cooperating)

GROUP

TEACHER-
DIRECTED
(lecture,
demonstration)

STUDENT-
CENTERED
(discussion,
discoverry)

INDIVIDUAL

PRODUCT
(knowledge, skills, focusing on the concrete)

CONCEPTS AND CHOICES • presenter knowledge, preparation, and skill • student preparation, motivation, and skills • degree of teacher enthusiasm and student engagement • student participation • meaningfulness of materials and activities • a positive climate • quality of instructional time • quality of feedback

---

Comments/Notes/
Plans/Reflections:

	(low)	(high)
Presenter Knowledge	1 2 3 4 5	
Presenter Preparation	1 2 3 4 5	
Presenter Enthusiasm/Energy	1 2 3 4 5	
Presenter Organization	1 2 3 4 5	
Presenter Clarity	1 2 3 4 5	
Student Engagement	1 2 3 4 5	
Content/Activity Meaningfulness	1 2 3 4 5	
Positive Learning Climate	1 2 3 4 5	

If applicable:

Feedback to Students	1 2 3 4 5
Check for Understanding	1 2 3 4 5
Appropriateness of Assessment	1 2 3 4 5
Availability of Practice	1 2 3 4 5
Preview/Review/Closure	1 2 3 4 5
Surface/Deep Learning	1 2 3 4 5
Effects of Class size, Room Layout, Audiovisual Use	1 2 3 4 5

Bloom's Taxonomy

Knowledge	1 2 3 4 5
Comprehension	1 2 3 4 5
Application	1 2 3 4 5
Analysis	1 2 3 4 5
Synthesis	1 2 3 4 5
Evaluation	1 2 3 4 5

Overall Course/ Presentation Challenge	1 2 3 4 5

Additional notes, etc.:

STUDENT REFLECTIONS
ABOUT LEARNING AND INSTRUCTION

Teacher/Course: Date:

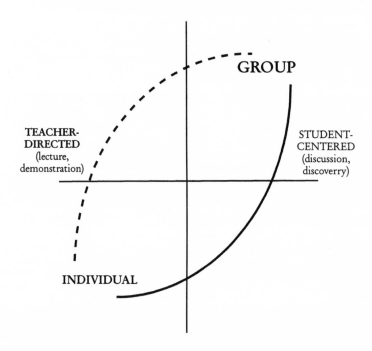

PROCESS
(thinking, working with abstractions, creating,
communicating, cooperating)

GROUP

**TEACHER-
DIRECTED**
(lecture,
demonstration)

**STUDENT-
CENTERED**
(discussion,
discovery)

INDIVIDUAL

PRODUCT
(knowledge, skills, focusing on the concrete)

CONCEPTS AND CHOICES • presenter knowledge, preparation, and skill • student preparation, motivation, and skills • degree of presenter enthusiasm and student engagement • student participation • meaningfulness of materials and activities • a positive climate • quality of instructional time • quality of feedback

---

	Comments/Notes/ *Plans/Reflections:*
	Impact on YOUR learning
	(low) (high)
Presenter Knowledge	1 2 3 4 5
Presenter Preparation	1 2 3 4 5
Presenter Enthusiasm/Energy	1 2 3 4 5
Presenter Organization	1 2 3 4 5
Presenter Clarity	1 2 3 4 5
Student Engagement	1 2 3 4 5
Content/Activity Meaningfulness	1 2 3 4 5
Positive Learning Climate	1 2 3 4 5

If applicable:

Feedback to Students	1 2 3 4 5
Check for Understanding	1 2 3 4 5
Appropriateness of Assessment	1 2 3 4 5
Availability of Practice	1 2 3 4 5
Preview/Review/Closure	1 2 3 4 5
Surface/Deep Learning	1 2 3 4 5
Effects of Class size, Room Layout, Audiovisual Use	1 2 3 4 5

Bloom's Taxonomy

Knowledge	1 2 3 4 5
Comprehension	1 2 3 4 5
Application	1 2 3 4 5
Analysis	1 2 3 4 5
Synthesis	1 2 3 4 5
Evaluation	1 2 3 4 5

Overall Course/ Presentation Challenge	1 2 3 4 5

Martin Luther King, Jr.

There is so much in the life of Dr. Martin Luther King, Jr., that continues to inspire me, but the memories of being in the audience one autumn evening in 1964 for one of his rallies still brings chills — he was that powerful.

I was part of a large crowd at a local high school in Cambridge, Massachusetts, there to provide vocal and financial support for Dr. King's work for integration in the South. I was in my first year of college, unsure of my place in the world but hyper-alert to the burgeoning Civil Rights movement. On this particular night, I was able to suspend my so very hyper-rationality, conditioned through too many years of obedient and prescribed schooling, and instead allow myself to be caught up in something very big — something right and compelling for the highest of moral principles.

We were all electrified by his words and emotion. His voice echoed off the walls in cadences filled with reason and resonance, appeal and inspiration, swelling with the crowd's voluntary calls back: "Amen!" "Tell it, Brother King." "Hallelujah!" The room shook as spirits lifted, soared. No speech before or since has ever come close to matching that special evening for me.

Even rereading some of his other speeches still reminds me of King's continuing hold on my psyche. For example, I've often criticized the gatekeeping function of some teachers and the inevitable casualties when exams are graded on a curve, when student talent and hopes are discouraged through unnecessary competition and excessive failure. I've thought of King when I've tried instead to focus on student interdependence, on the support and assistance students can give each other when we teachers help nurture a learning community. Sometimes I need to step back and remind myself of certain core goals. Think about King's (1984, 18) message in the following:

> All [people] are interdependent. Every nation is an heir of a vast treasury of ideas and labor to which both the living and the dead of all nations have contributed. Whether we realize it or not, each of us lives eternally in the 'red.' We are everlasting debtors to known and unknown men and women. When we arise in the morning, we go into the bathroom where we reach for the sponge which is provided for us by a Pacific Islander. We reach for soap which is created for us by a European. Then at the table we drink coffee which is provided for us by a South American, or tea by a Chinese, or cocoa by a West African. Before we leave for our jobs we are already beholden to more than half the world.

King always seemed to think big. I hope the *Instructional Map* can help you step back so that you can stay mindful of that bigger picture when you teach.

Here's another example: When I struggle with student apathy, when I want students' fires to ignite and their energies to awaken, while I may have what I think is much of value to pass on, I often must remind myself of the need for my students to be active in the process of *constructing* meaning for themselves if a deeper learning is to take place. I then find value in these words from another King speech (1984, 19):

> When an individual is no longer a true participant, ... (when) culture is degraded, ... when the social system does not build security but induces peril, inexorably the individual is impelled to pull away from a soulless society. This process produces alienation — perhaps the most pervasive and insidious development in contemporary society.

I then look at the *Instructional Map* and wonder what I can do at the student end of the continuum to evoke more of their energies, their investment.

When I challenge myself to cross the great divide between teaching and learning, to question my own effectiveness when some percentage of students do poorly, I find inspiration in King's call to persevere, to struggle. Can even the Nobel laureate rest if his or her students are failing (King 1984, 21)?

> As long as there is poverty in the world I can never be rich, even if I have a billion dollars. As long as diseases are rampant and millions of people in this world cannot expect to live more than twenty-eight or thirty years, I can never be totally healthy, even if I just got a good checkup at Mayo Clinic. I can never be what I ought to be until you are what you ought to be. This is the way the world is made. No individual or nation can stand out boasting of being independent. We are interdependent.

But what can we realistically do as teachers when some students continue to disappoint us — when some can't seem to understand the material or others seem to care so little for their studies? As King (1984, 25) insists:

> We must accept finite disappointment, but we must never lose infinite hope. ... I have the audacity to believe that peoples everywhere can have three meals a day for their bodies, education and culture for their minds, and dignity, equality, and freedom for their spirits. I believe that what self-centered men have torn down, other-centered [people] can build up.

If nothing else, we have to be able to stand back from the instructional process and keep hope alive for ourselves and our students.

When I use the *Instructional Map* to try to find my way through to the right balance of knowledge and thinking for own my courses, that mix of information and activity that allows students to think more critically and creatively, I am buoyed by these words from King (1984, 41):

> Education must enable one to sift and weigh evidence, to discern the true from the false, the real from the unreal, and the facts from fiction. The function of education, therefore, is to teach one to think intensively and critically. ... We must remember that intelligence is not enough. Intelligence plus character — that is the goal of true education. The complete education gives one not only power of concentration but worthy objectives upon which to concentrate.

Rereading these words inevitably gives me courage to work more at the process end of the *Instructional Map,* challenging students to broaden their ideas, sharpen their analytical skills, and deepen their understanding.

When I need another reminder of the bigger picture, the work ahead and the patience I will need to push for needed improvements, I can also reflect on the following words from Dr. King (1984, 59):

> Human progress is neither automatic nor inevitable. Even a superficial look at history reveals that no social advance rolls in on wheels of inevitability. Every step toward the goal of justice requires sacrifice, suffering, and struggle, the tireless exertions and passionate concerns of dedicated individuals. ... This is no time for apathy or complacency. This is a time for vigorous and positive action.

Amen, Brother King.

CHAPTER 7

THE
Instructional Map
AND various
Instructional
Approaches

In what follows, I provide a brief overview of various instructional approaches and then illustrate each using an *Instructional Map*.

Bloom's Taxonomy

Many teachers find Benjamin Bloom's (1956) taxonomy of objectives in the cognitive domain helpful for a variety of reasons — for planning, guiding their own questions and the discussions that follow, or developing balanced test items reflecting a range of intellectual challenge. Building on knowledge at the lowest level, learners engage in qualitatively different kinds of thinking as they move through understanding, application, analysis, synthesis, and evaluation.

The film *Stand and Deliver* chronicles the story of Jaime Escalante (played by Edward James Olmos), who left a comfortable position in the aerospace industry to teach math at Garfield High School, which was located in one of the poorest and roughest sections of East Los Angeles. Defying the low expectations of the community and other staff members, Escalante helped his students perform so well on advanced placement exams that he was investigated by the Educational Testing Service for suspicion of falsifying test score results. Forced to take the test again, his students, in true Hollywood fashion, vindicated themselves famously.

In one classic scene that illustrates the use of Bloom's taxonomy, Escalante is seen drilling his students (a task at the lowest cognitive level) about the number line:

> A negative times a negative is a positive. Say it again. All together. A negative times a negative is a positive. Again. A negative times a negative is a positive. Again. A negative times a negative is a positive. Why?

Dead silence reigns. He pauses, watches. The scene shifts. To create that moment of reflection, Escalante asked "why?" to move the focus from drill and practice at the *knowledge* level to the next higher level, a demand for *understanding*.

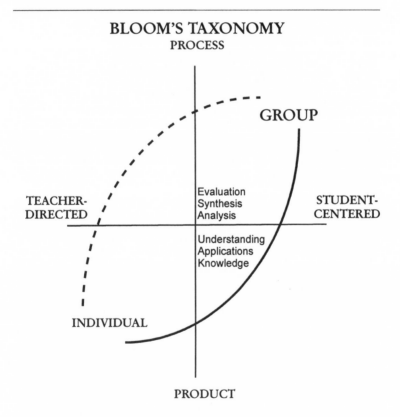

BLOOM'S TAXONOMY
PROCESS

GROUP

TEACHER-
DIRECTED

Evaluation
Synthesis
Analysis

STUDENT-
CENTERED

Understanding
Applications
Knowledge

INDIVIDUAL

PRODUCT

Teachers can make use of this hierarchy to plan lessons, guide discussions, develop exams, and more.

Or think of the Robin Williams character, John Keating, in the film *Dead Poets Society.* Hired to teach English literature at an elite prep school, Keating memorialized the Latin phrase "carpe diem" — "seize the day." Challenging his students to make their lives extraordinary, Keating goes for the higher-order intellectual levels of *analysis, synthesis,* and *evaluation.* In one memorable scene, he takes the students from their classroom to the wood-paneled room where the pictures of Welton School graduates hang. There, Keating insists that they look at those photographs from the past and think about their lives to be. His words to them are roughly as follows:

> They're not that different from any of you, are they? There's hope in their eyes, just like in yours. They believe themselves destined for wonderful things, just like many of you. Well, where are those smiles now, boys? What of that hope? You see, these boys are pushing up daisies. They're food for worms. Did they make their lives extraordinary?

As you look at the *Instructional Map* that follows, with Bloom's hierarchy superimposed on the product-process axis, think of Escalante's class described above, or Keating's, or a recent class of your own. Think of the cognitive demands. What could have made your class better? More challenging? Or did your students lack the necessary foundation of facts and skills to be able to perform the higher-order tasks?

You can address each of these levels from your role as teacher. Or you can have students work with ideas on their own or in small groups. Centering activities on the right side of the *Instructional Map,* where student-centered activities occur, can be very useful for allowing students to *practice* the ideas and skills you're discussing. Because it's difficult to objectively assess student thinking (analysis, synthesis, and evaluation) when you want to work in the upper-right quadrant, activities like cooperative problem solving can prove valuable by giving you opportunities to observe students and listen to their reasoning. Here again, you can use Bloom's taxonomy as a lens for analyzing and evaluating student responses.

Positive Learning Climate

Let's use the *Instructional Map* to illustrate the role of *learning climate* — e.g., student morale, mutual respect, trust, opportunities for student input — in supporting the learning process. While some instructors put all of their energies into content coverage, others find that they can improve learning and create higher-quality interactions by enhancing student motivation.

Connecting student morale to learning

Much solid research now connects the climate in your classroom with the quality of student learning (e.g., Fox et al. 1974; Lezotte et al. 1980; Lowman 1995; Shaheen and Patrick 1974). This should come as no surprise. Taking time from content coverage to bolster morale may enhance the quality of the instructional time you have with students, securing deeper engagement and more willing participation from them.

Let's look at an example. I like to take time for introductions at the start of each semester so that students in a particular class can feel like they're part of a community. Even in large classes I try to orchestrate opportunities for students to discuss their responses to a particular question. I will often ask them to come to consensus, write down their responses, sign their names to them, and turn them in at the end of class. This gives students a few moments to work together on ideas presented in class, which promotes more active learning and critical thinking. It also helps break down barriers between and among students, the distance and isolation they have from each other, especially in large classes.

Soliciting input from everyone involved

Another important aspect of a positive classroom climate is the degree to which you can involve students in decisions affecting them. Taking stock of everyone's feelings and experiences a few weeks into the semester gives you a chance to make course modifications while the semester is still in progress, a process William Glasser (e.g., 1969, 1975, 1986, 1992) refers to as the *classroom meeting*. I'm always taken by how appreciative students are when teachers stop to consult with them about their learning, about what's working and possible course improvements. When I've facilitated feedback sessions for colleagues, students will invariably thank me for the opportunity; I quickly remind these students to thank the teacher who invited me. This can be a real morale boost for any course, especially as the semester moves past the halfway point, as exams and assignments come due, and as the inevitable wrinkles appear in the class fabric — wrinkles that you can iron out with some talk and attention.

Darrel Fontane teaches an engineering course. He once asked me in to facilitate a mid-semester feedback session, in part because he wanted some early evaluation of various innovations he had initiated, and in part because he wanted to model for students what was standard practice in the field when those involved with a

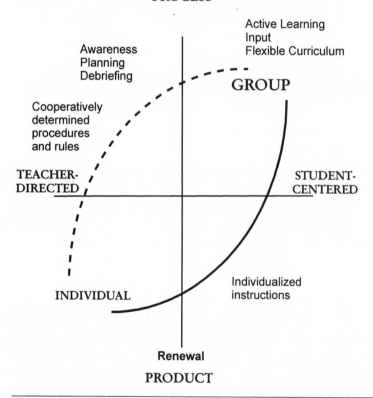

POSITIVE CLIMATE

PROCESS

Active Learning
Input
Flexible Curriculum

Awareness
Planning
Debriefing

GROUP

Cooperatively
determined
procedures
and rules

TEACHER-DIRECTED

STUDENT-CENTERED

INDIVIDUAL

Individualized
instructions

Renewal

PRODUCT

Foundation of trust, mutual respect, care, growth, high morale, cohesiveness, variety, support, and more.

Notes:

particular project gather periodically to take stock of progress made, acknowledge what's working, and address any concerns that exist. What was fascinating for me as the facilitator was the degree to which students were willing to take time from the course content to join in a very rich discussion about learning, discussing what was the best use of class time and where the teacher's expertise would be most valuable.

Building trust with mutual respect and caring

When I can, I will vary introductions and ask students to describe themselves as, for example, a vehicle or an animal. This is a common trust-building exercise in which students can reveal much about their core self-concepts. When I describe myself as an older Volvo station wagon, for example, I hear my own values for dependability and quality. When I describe myself as a panther, I notice my lean toward independence and strength. It makes for a fun introduction, and everyone knows everyone else a bit better afterward. This kind of process tends to be much more memorable than the more conventional, "Tell us your name, major, hometown, etc."

Program, process, and material determinants.

There are specific features (or "determinants") of instruction that researchers have associated with a positive classroom climate.

Program determinants are:
- active learning,
- individualized instruction,
- varied environments,
- a flexible curriculum,
- support, and
- rules that are cooperatively determined.

Process determinants, on the other hand, are:
- problem solving abilities,
- instructional goals,
- conflicts that are identified and worked on,
- effective communication involving those affected in decision making,
- a mixture of autonomy and accountability,
- effective instructional strategies, and
- an ability to plan for the future.

Researchers have also identified *material* determinants, which support a positive climate for teaching and learning:

- adequate resources,
- a responsive support system, and
- a suitable physical space.

Cognitive Development

Looking at learning from a developmental perspective can mean a radical switch in your approach to teaching, with, for example, much more attention to student learning and errors. To promote a deeper understanding, you may transmit less information directly in class and do more to facilitate active student learning. You may actually "teach" less (in a formal sense), but observe, listen, interact, and assess more.

For example, when it means a richer and more stimulating learning environment, you may decide that group work will take precedence over individual study.

Look through the brief descriptions below and see how I organize them on the *Instructional Map* that follows. While the map contains references to Piaget's ground-breaking work, other developmentalists who are mentioned in the text could be portrayed in a similar manner.

A sequence of developmental stages

Developmentalists like Piaget, Perry, Kohlberg, Gilligan, Erikson, Rogoff, and Tharp describe the qualitative shifts that occur in human thinking with maturation, experience, and learning. As a teacher, you can be more attentive to the specific stages that define student development and try to create challenges that can then serve as catalysts for deeper reflection and growth among your students. Remember that this process is gradual and centered upon the student; any conclusions you reach will be purely inferential.

Shifts happen!

Piaget described shifts in thinking that help students handle increasingly abstract material, manipulate symbols (linguistic or mathematical), and use more sophisticated logical processes. Both Piaget and Perry reported a shift from more egocentric thinking to an openness to the opinions and beliefs of others. Research into

moral development led some scholars to similar hierarchies. However, while Kohlberg insisted that ethical principles were at the
highest level of his model, Gilligan alerted us to the tendency among
females to pay more attention to relationships. Erikson, in turn,
noted shifts in underlying motivations across the lifespan.

In the *Instructional Map* that follows, I try to illustrate the key
concepts and practices that guide my own thinking about developmental principles and their value for teaching.

PIAGET AND COGNITIVE DEVELOPMENT

PROCESS

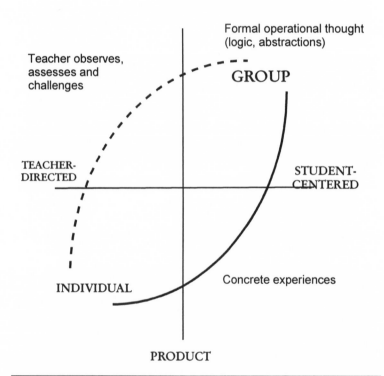

PRODUCT

A developmental perspective which builds on the work of Piaget stresses
concrete experiences and hands-on learning for students as a foundation
for more conceptual and abstract thinking. Teachers establish
stimulating environments, observe and assess learning, and challenge
students to think more abstractly.

A developmental perspective that builds on the work of Piaget stresses concrete experiences and hands-on learning for students as a foundation for more conceptual and abstract thinking. The teacher establishes a stimulating environment, observes and assesses learning, and challenges students to think more abstractly.

William Perry, Jr.

Although Piaget's work focuses more on the development of thinking in infants and adolescents, it does have relevance for young adults, especially in its description of more sophisticated logic in the *formal operational* stage. William Perry's (1981) model, however, builds on the work of Piaget and other developmentalists and focuses specifically on cognitive development in the college-age student.

According to Perry, students entering college right out of high school, at age eighteen or so, tend to think primarily in dualistic terms — answers are right or wrong, and situations are good or bad. At this stage, knowledge itself is quantitative, measurable. What Perry terms *agency*, or the source of truth, is external for these students, attributed to the teacher and/or the textbook. At this stage, students lack confidence in their own thinking. By insisting on right answers and the referencing of experts, schools reinforce this sense of external agency.

With time and exposure to increasingly complex problems or issues, students begin to recognize the variety of approaches or viewpoints that exist. This stage can make for a kind of *naive openness*, a positive shift from a more rigid type of thinking but still relatively uncritical of other perspectives. With increasingly sophisticated thinking, however, students enter what Perry terms the stage of *relativism*, where they put differing opinions and ideas under a more critical light and examine each for reliability and validity. Disagreements become possible. At this stage, students look for the coherence of supporting evidence. Knowledge becomes more context-dependent, more qualitative, dependent upon the ways in which the data are organized and the "spin" that gets added.

According to Perry, students at the highest stage are able to reflect upon and deepen their own beliefs. In his terms, *agency* becomes *internal*, and students examine new ideas in a systematic and thoughtful manner. Using Piaget's notions, students can either *assimilate* (accept) new ideas within their existing thought structures or actually *accommodate* (or change) what they believe.

For example, one useful activity for postsecondary teachers and students is to analyze the content of any exam for its fit with Perry's model. If all of your questions are at the *knowledge* level, where there is a focus on mastery or correctness (i.e., dichotomous thinking), you may want to ask questions at higher levels to challenge students to consider other possibilities and then articulate and defend their beliefs. In Bloom's terms, you ask students to understand, analyze, synthesize, and evaluate.

PERRY'S MODEL

PROCESS

Commitment
Relativism
Multiplicity

Teacher observes, assesses, challenges

GROUP

TEACHER-DIRECTED

STUDENT-CENTERED

INDIVIDUAL

Dualistic thinking

PRODUCT

Teachers can assess student comments for indication of the level of student thinking. Exposing students to the model itself can promote metacognitive capacity where students themselves are more aware of their own thinking processes. Try using empathy to help students with frustration.

Steve Shulman is a professor of economics who shuns simplistic answers to real-world complexities. When discussing the various arguments offered about welfare reform, for example, he will help students see the logic behind each. When I asked one student to describe Shulman as a teacher, she said:

> Just when I think I know his position, when I have him pegged, he'll jump to another place and give a good explanation of some other viewpoint. He's very challenging that way. He really forces me to get past my guessing game about what he thinks and get deeper into my own thinking.

Not surprisingly, Shulman uses an essay format for exams. It's more labor-intensive for him to grade, of course, but he believes this approach is much more likely to stimulate students' thinking.

Problem-Based Learning

Problem-based learning (or *case-based learning*) is an approach to instruction that is gaining increasing popularity in some parts of higher education, especially in fields like medicine, where students will eventually move into roles calling for a great deal of critical and creative thinking about real and inevitably complex problems.

Because these roles defy overly reductionistic reasoning (e.g., Barrows and Tamblyn 1980), teachers help students learn how to access a range of sources and think through various issues. When compared with a more traditional, linear transmission of knowledge via lecture, a problem-based format addresses course content through a more guided, holistic immersion, with much less predictable outcomes.

Student-centered

In the problem-based approach, teachers pose problems, students do the needed research, and together teachers and students explore possibilities. As the teacher, you become a facilitator of understanding, setting the stage, raising questions, probing responses, guiding discussions, and challenging assumptions, all in an attempt to sharpen and deepen student thinking. While your own expertise may feel tested by the range of issues that emerge, you may also feel challenged by the requirements of the discussion process itself — for example, how to sustain wide participation and interest among your students.

Debriefing the process

While you help students stay focused on key concepts, debriefing the process when it's over can help your students think about their own thinking and consider alternatives. You can review which lines of reasoning seemed most useful and which were not, who contributed what and when, and to what extent the process paralleled what occurs in the field.

PROBLEM-BASED LEARNING

PROCESS

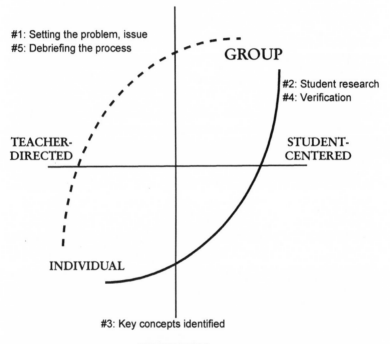

#1: Setting the problem, issue
#5: Debriefing the process

GROUP

#2: Student research
#4: Verification

TEACHER-DIRECTED

STUDENT-CENTERED

INDIVIDUAL

#3: Key concepts identified

PRODUCT

Teachers present students with problems and then guide their efforts at solutions. Closely modeled on work in the field, this approach is high on relevance, student engagement, critical and creative thinking.

Notes:

Jamie Gaynor and Pete Hellyer have experimented with a problem-based approach in their section on anesthesiology for second-year students in the veterinary program at Colorado State University. Compared with a more traditional lecture approach, which moves in a more direct way through the curriculum, Gaynor and Hellyer set out the challenge or "mystery" — the symptoms and circumstances associated with a particular case — and then guide students through a diagnosis and treatment plan. Questions are raised and debated, and students are often polled before the instructors offer their best judgment. The pace is fast yet punctuated with marked periods of silence as students wrestle with difficult decisions.

Mastery Learning

You can think of *mastery learning* as an applied "science of instruction." Utilizing much that research has documented about learning specific kinds of information or skills, instructors can design and manage their teaching in ways that practically guarantee success for every student who is willing to do the work required. Typically, a mastery learning approach involves much *less* direct instruction and much *more* individualized or small-group learning, with frequent opportunities for assessment and feedback.

Standards and success

Fundamental to the mastery learning approach is a clear set of standards that define mastery. These standards are then broken down into sub-goals and measurable learning objectives so that you and your students can know how far along they are at any point in time. It's no longer a matter of "seat time" or just attending class. Students can test out of any component or, conversely, repeat their studies until they demonstrate mastery.

Unfortunately, this instructional "safety net" can also lower motivation for those students who "need" the pressure of an upcoming exam, the competition for a good grade if the course is graded on a curve, or even the threat of failure. Conversely, while success can be a wonderful elixir for those students who are struggling, your time and energy may be stretched as you search for ways to ensure learning.

A sequence of instruction

Along with clear standards and a focus on success, the mastery learning approach requires a careful sequencing of instruction, so that student learning proceeds in logical and manageable steps. As the instructor, you have the pivotal role in designing this sequence and its linkages.

All of this may sound very appealing, rational, and sensible; after all, who can argue with something described as the "science of instruction"? Yet the burden is on you to create and manage what amounts to a very student-centered approach to instruction. There is often a lot of record keeping involved: quizzes, assignments, repeat exams, and so on. Some commercially becoming available products are available to lend a hand (e.g., Web CT has a component that gives students results on practice quizzes as well as those that they want counted toward their grades).

Teaching and modeling

Because there is such a focus on tested mastery under this approach, what you do as a teacher is largely determined by your goals, learning objectives, and assessment procedures. You are teaching to the tests for all intents and purposes, helping students master what they need to know. To support what you tell your students, most mastery models mix in a heavy dose of modeling. After telling students what they need to do, it is often helpful to show them — to demonstrate the skills they will need and the procedures you use.

Practice

Also essential to mastery are opportunities for students to work with the ideas and skills under study as they develop and deepen their understanding of them. At first under your supervision but then increasingly on their own, students work toward independence. As the teacher, you can shift from presenter to observer and mentor, managing a process similar to an apprenticeship.

Feedback and assessment

Also fundamental to mastery learning is the teacher's ongoing attention to student progress — checking regularly for understanding (e.g., questions, observations, discussions, assignments) and carrying out more formal evaluations (e.g., quizzes, exams, papers, projects). You and your students need to know what *they* know and don't know; it is this knowledge that informs your decisions about further instruction and the students' understanding of their own progress.

Frequent assessments promote student success and minimize misunderstandings. There is a greater teacher-student-curriculum

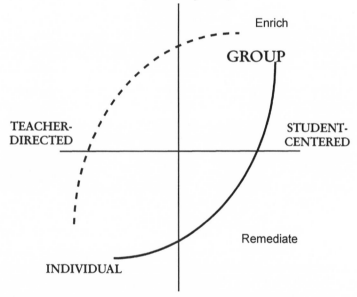

Mastery Learning

PROCESS

Teach ↔ Model ↔ Guided Practice ↔ Practice ↔ Assess
(more subjective)

Enrich

GROUP

TEACHER-DIRECTED

STUDENT-CENTERED

Remediate

INDIVIDUAL

Teach ↔ Model ↔ Guided Practice ↔ Practice ↔ Assess
(more objective)

PRODUCT

Teachers carefully sequence instruction, setting clear and achievable standards, providing frequent checks for understanding, and, hopefully, guaranteeing success for nearly all students.

Notes:

alignment when students are clear about your expectations. Additionally, you get frequent input into their struggles and successes, data that can help you make needed adjustments. It bears repeating, however, that all of this requires time and effort. In addition, the focus on measurable output can detract from intrinsic interests the students may have.

In a new course for first-year students, Gailmarie Kimmel and I have attempted to apply aspects of mastery learning to help students develop better study habits through focused effort and success. We require an extensive rewriting process before collecting the final copy of a five-page autobiographical paper on themselves as "learners within a sustainable community." Students must have readers offer written feedback on each of two earlier drafts and submit these along with their rewritten copy. While some students have complained about the work required, most have appreciated the opportunity to incorporate feedback and refine their first efforts.

A mastery learning approach takes much of the guesswork out of teaching and permits students to learn from their earlier mistakes, using your comments more as feedback and less as final judgment. Having students solicit feedback from others — in our case, from classmates or the staff of the University Writing Center — eases the burden on us and makes for much better final copy when we need to assign grades.

Creativity

Helping students develop their creative capacities can add much fun and energy to your courses while nurturing student abilities that are too often neglected. Writers like Alvin Toffler (1980), Roger von Oeck (1983, 1986), and Tom Peters (1987) argue that creativity represents skills and ideas that are increasingly important. Yet few instructors know what to do with these qualities in the classroom. Can we teach creativity? When do we stop building a foundation of knowledge and start asking students to use their newly learned information to think in new ways?

Creativity is one of those constructs that we place in the upper regions of the product-process continuum within the *Instructional Map*. Once you understand some of the basic concepts underlying creativity and how they may play out in your classroom, you can find any number of ways to add something innovative to your teaching — perhaps new and different content, or an activity or assignment that can really stretch students' thinking.

Tapping the nonrational

Central to the development of creativity is your ability to help students develop their *nonrational* capabilities for learning — their emotional resources, their intuition, and their willingness to take risks, to see things from different perspectives, and to be open to

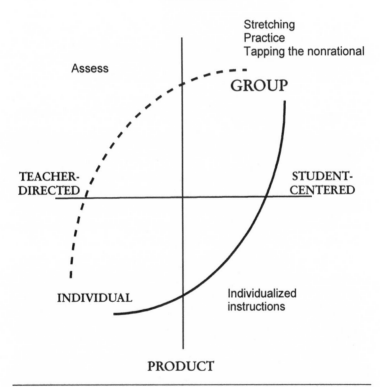

CREATIVITY

PROCESS

Stretching
Practice
Tapping the nonrational

Assess

GROUP

**TEACHER-
DIRECTED**

**STUDENT-
CENTERED**

INDIVIDUAL

Individualized
instructions

PRODUCT

Teachers transform their value for creativity into practice sessions and assignments where students are stretched to tap nonrational capabilities, us analogies, metaphors, etc.

Notes:

change. Challenging students to break through conventional ways of thinking, you can expose them to the use of analogies and metaphors, for example — how other things or ideas can serve as useful models for rethinking projects and problems. With your guidance, students can learn to use those "things" to evoke different feelings and ideas, which can then be brought to bear on old problems as well as new ones.

Practice as stretching

Because of the inherently subjective nature of creativity, agreeing on clear outcomes for student learning is problematic. What you can do, however, is create opportunities for students to stretch their usual ways of responding, to tap into "other" capacities, and to practice being creative. Accordingly, your assessment of their efforts will be largely subjective, reflecting your own judgment of their success at introducing new and innovative thinking.

Nanci Erskine frequently presses her introductory drawing students to see the world differently — for example, to squint and literally change what they see. Or she herself will take a slide and manipulate the focus on the projector to make a more blurred image. Once, as I watched, it seemed like a process of "artistic deconstruction" as Erskine challenged the prevailing student "perceptual canon." While this process initially frustrated some students who wanted to concentrate on their more developed talents, everyone with whom I talked eventually came to appreciate the new worlds and possibilities that opened up through this kind of exploration.

Discovery Learning

One of the more challenging approaches to teaching, *discovery learning* or inquiry, attempts to foster critical and creative thinking, to help students better understand their own thinking processes (metacognition), and to give students experiences with problem solving in which answers may be complex and in which different perspectives and approaches are possible. While interest in discovery learning has grown with the move toward *constructivist* learning, its earlier appearance followed the almost hysterical American preoccupation with the Soviet launching of Sputnik in 1957 and a perceived vital need to train more scientists or, short of that, to help students think more like scientists. Hence, the focus on discovery.

Posing problems or puzzling issues can prove highly engaging for students, challenging for teachers as well and energizing for everyone involved. To be good at it, you will need skill and artistry, an eye for discriminating productive from unproductive activities, and tolerance for ambiguity and its accompanying frustrations.

Engaging student interest

To begin an inquiry lesson, you will need a problem or puzzle. In practice, discovery learning looks very similar to problem-based learning. Both approaches flow from similar goals and research bases. Both approaches go for student engagement at the outset. One subtle difference, however, may be the extent to which problem-based learning is more focused on content — the problem or cases and the learnings that result — while discovery learning has traditionally given more attention to students as learners and to students' abilities to think critically: to understand, apply, analyze, synthesize, and evaluate; to solve problems; to consider various strategies; and to reflect on paths taken or ignored.

Rekindling curiosity

One underlying hope with the discovery learning process is that students will rediscover their own intrinsic interests. We all possess a natural curiosity as children, but our own interests often get routed, shaped, conditioned, and, all too often, stifled through years of formal schooling. Focusing on student inquiry will get you away from a strict focus on course coverage and thinking more about relevance and meaning from a student perspective.

Handling ambiguity and complexity

With discovery learning also comes an emphasis on both the intellectual and emotional demands of problem solving and creative risk taking. Once freed from strict adherence to teacher-supplied dictums and algorithms, students often need to relearn how to fend more for themselves. Add in the challenges of handling ambiguity and complexity and many students struggle with the openness and inevitable frustrations associated with discovery learning. Yet some students come alive with a challenge to discover, and that is one of the joys of this approach. Discovery can give you a very different perspective on your students. It has often changed my own notion of just who are my "best" students — of who will rise to the challenge and who will get paralyzed by the freedom.

The discovery process

The process for guiding a discovery lesson attempts to model what scientists do when they face unknowns in their own research areas. You can use the following steps as a general framework for attacking a problem:

1. Challenge students to define the problem.
2. Have students develop hypotheses.
3. Ask students to define and clarify those hypotheses.
4. Have students explore any assumptions made, the implications that arise from those assumptions, and the logical validity of their arguments.
5. Have students gather data.
6. Ask students to generalize their conclusions where possible.

The teacher as facilitator, guide, and resource

As a teacher using the discovery approach, you shift your focus from lecturer to facilitator, from presenter to observer. However, your expertise will be as important as ever, perhaps even more important. Countless questions may emerge from the process. You will have to be on your toes to keep the focus on student discovery while simultaneously juggling the demands of content coverage, and to answer what you can or point the way to other resources.

Debriefing the process

One component to discovery learning that is too often overlooked involves debriefing when you lead students in a discussion about the thinking they used (individually and in their groups) or about what worked and what didn't. With this kind of sharing and some opportunity for reflection, students are better able to consider new and different approaches in the future.

On two different campuses, physicists have told me how they often use a discovery approach to help students unlearn misconceptions about the physical world. Both Joel Primack (University of California-Santa Cruz) and Sandy Kern (Colorado State University) agree on the difficulty of undoing erroneous thinking through direct instruction. What you typically get when you resort to a frontal teaching "assault" are memorized responses, which only mask errors of understanding lurking beneath the surface. Alternatively, when you can challenge students with new data or insights inconsistent with their current ways of thinking, some cognitive dissonance can begin to stew, simmering over time into an openness to new ways of thinking and a refashioned understanding.

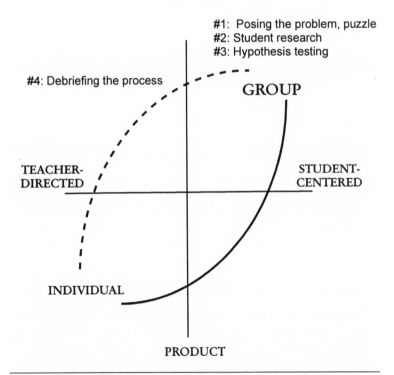

DISCOVERY LEARNING
PROCESS

#1: Posing the problem, puzzle
#2: Student research
#3: Hypothesis testing

#4: Debriefing the process

GROUP

TEACHER-
DIRECTED

STUDENT-
CENTERED

INDIVIDUAL

PRODUCT

Teachers engage students at the start, set out ground rules for the investigation, guide the process, provide clues as needed, point toward other resources and then conclude with a debriefing session.

Notes:

THE
Heart
for Teaching

In his very popular book, *The Courage to Teach,* Parker Palmer speaks to the rigors of teaching as well as the joys that emerge when we align our values with our actions and address the full human range of needs and hopes that students bring into class. Drawing on years of experience as a college instructor as well as more recent work as a full-time consultant on faculty development, Palmer appeals for much more than content coverage — for more that is holistic, that recognizes all that matters to both teachers and students and allows for the kind of rich interchange humans need.

It's rare for me to underline much in a book, but I did in this one. This book spoke so directly to me, my own teaching, and the work I do in faculty and instructional development. Consider Palmer's (1998, 1) opening lines:

> I am a teacher at heart, and there are moments in the
> classroom when I can hardly hold the joy. When my
> students and I discover uncharted territory to ex-
> plore, when the pathway out of a thicket opens up
> before us, when our experience is illumined by the
> lightning-life of the mind — then teaching is the finest
> work I know.

I hope the *Instructional Map* can help you find your own path through this dense and complex terrain of content, person, and place.

When analyzing the differences among teachers, Palmer (1998, 11) goes on to offer the following:

> Bad teachers distance themselves from the subject
> they are teaching — and in the process, from their

students. Good teachers join self and subject and students in the fabric of life.

Using the *Instructional Map* to hold the continua in front of you — being alert to the interactions among product (e.g., information), process (e.g., thinking), locus of instruction (teacher, student), and group size — can help you plan and teach in ways that reflect more of this rich dynamic without getting too lost on any one coordinate.

Looking then at the goals and objectives that guide teaching, Palmer (1998, 51) writes:

> If we regard truth as emerging from a complex process of mutual inquiry, the classroom will look like a resourceful and interdependent community. Our assumptions about knowing can open up, or shut down, the capacity for connectedness on which good teaching depends.

Instead of using only one classroom format, we can open up to a whole range of possibilities that allow for new and different expressions.

Further along in the book, Palmer (1998, 64) offers a provocative description of the competing factors that drive good teaching:

> What I want is a richer, more paradoxical model of teaching and learning than binary thought allows, a model that reveals how the paradox of thinking and feeling are joined — whether we are comfortable with paradox or not.

Using the *Instructional Map* may encourage you to think about these intersections before you ever begin to teach, when you are planning, or afterwards when you want to reflect on what happened. Having your *Map* with you in class can also alert you to these dynamics without your getting lost in any one direction.

This "paradoxical" model of teaching and learning lets Palmer (1998, 66) address a number of issues in nondichotomous ways:

> The world of education as we know it is filled with broken paradoxes — and with the lifeless results:
>
> - We separate head from heart. ...
> - We separate facts from feelings. Result: bloodless facts that make the world distant and remote and ignorant emotions that reduce truth to how one feels today.

- We separate theory from practice. ...
- We separate teaching from learning. Result: teachers who talk but do not listen and students who listen but do not talk.

Paradoxical thinking requires that we embrace a view of the world in which opposites are joined, so that we can see the world clearly and see it whole. Such a view is characterized by neither flinty-eyed realism nor dewey-eyed romanticism but rather by a creative synthesis of the two. ... When we think things together, we reclaim the life force in the world, in our students, in ourselves.

But just how do these imperatives translate into practical terms? Palmer (1998, 74) goes on to describe how he plans for his own teaching:

When I design a classroom session, I am aware of six paradoxical tensions that I want to build into the teaching and learning space. ...

1. The space should be bounded and open.
2. The space should be hospitable and "charged."
3. The space should invite the voice of the individual and the voice of the group.
4. The space should honor the "little" stories of the students and the "big" stories of the disciplines and tradition.
5. The space should support solitude and surround it with the resources of community.
6. The space should welcome both silence and speech.

The *Instructional Map* can help you stay alert to these factors and increase your ability to move in a particular direction as the content and conditions dictate.

Listen to Palmer's (1998, 133) further description of his planning process:

I must define the course in a way more engaging than engorging, countering my tendency to inundate students with data, and allowing them instead to encounter the subject, each other, and themselves. I must provide readings with substance that students need to know, but with gaps in which students can think their own thoughts. ... I must create exercises that invite students to probe the unknown, as well as exercises that reveal what they have learned. I must establish a schedule that allows time for the unexpected, even as it makes time to acquire the predictably necessary facts.

These intentions make for a very tall teaching order, but one that can be made more comprehensible when you check with your *Instructional Map* and note what you accomplished on a particular day. For example, you may have digressed during a particular session and covered less than you'd wanted, but the quality of student thinking may have been worth the effort. You may have spent more time than you had originally planned in small groups because the level of student engagement was so high. Or you may have wanted to clarify certain points yourself, only to realize the value in students' debating and discussing more with each other, ultimately sorting out more for themselves after hearing a range of viewpoints.

Near the end of *The Courage to Teach*, Palmer (1998, 147) makes his own reference to mapping when he describes how he leads teachers toward a deeper understanding of their most important classroom experiences:

> With this complex map before us, we understand something that makes our work more daunting but more intriguing: though teaching sometimes feels like a linear flow of experience from one session to the next, it is actually an intricate patterning of life, with rhythms, textures, and shapes we must attend to, a kind of creative chaos we can learn to enjoy. ... [By meeting together to discuss our experiences, we] have created a conversation that works like a navigator's triangulation, allowing us to locate ourselves more precisely on teaching's inner terrain by noting the position of others — without anyone's being told that he or she should move to a new location.

I hope the *Instructional Map* helps you find those bearings — whatever the weather, wind, or destination.

References

Ausubel, D.P. 1963. *The psychology of meaningful verbal learning: An introduction to school learning.* New York: Grune & Stratton.

Barrows, H.S., & Tamblyn, R.M. 1980. Problem-based learning: An approach to medical education. New York: Springer Publishing Co.

Bloom, B.S. 1956. *Taxonomy of educational objectives, handbook I: Cognitive domain.* New York: Longmans, Green.

Bloom, B.S. 1973. *Every kid can: Learning for mastery.* Washington, DC: College University Press.

Bruner, J.S. 1966. *Toward a theory of instruction.* Cambridge, MA: Belknap Press of Harvard University.

Bruner, J.S., Goodnow, J.J., & Austin, G.A. 1962. *A study of thinking.* New York: Science Editions.

Cameron, J. 1992. *The artist's way: A spiritual path to higher creativity.* New York: Tarcher/Putnam.

Carroll, J. 1963. A model of school learning. *Teachers College Record, 64,* 723-733.

Crum, T.F. 1997. *Journey to center: Lessons in unifying body, mind, and spirit.* New York: Fireside.

Csikszentmihalyi, M. 1990. *Flow: The psychology of optimal experience.* New York: HarperPerennial.

Erikson, E.H. 1974. *Dimensions of a new identity.* New York: W.W. Norton & Company.

Fox, R., Boies, H., Brainard, L., Fletcher, E., Huge, J., Logan, C., Schmuck, R., Shaheen, T., & Stegeman, W. 1974. *School climate improvement: A challenge to the school administrator.* Bloomington, IN: Phi Delta Kappa.

Freire, P. 1970. *Pedagogy of the oppressed.* New York: Continuum.

Gagné, R.M. 1985. *The conditions of learning and theory of instruction,* 4th ed. New York: Holt, Rinehart, & Winston.

Gagné, R.M., Briggs, L.J., & Wager, W.W. 1988. *Principles of instructional design.* San Francisco: Holt, Rinehart & Winston.

Gilligan, C. 1982. *In a different voice: Psychological theory and women's development.* Cambridge, MA: Harvard University Press.

Glasser, W. 1969. *Schools without failure.* New York: Harper & Row.

Glasser, W. 1975. *Reality therapy.* New York: Harper & Row.

Glasser, W. 1986. *Control theory in the classroom.* New York: Perennial Library.

Glasser, W. 1992. *The quality school: Managing students without coercion.* New York: HarperPerennial.

Gordon, W.J.J. 1961. *Synectics: The development of creative capacity.* New York: Harper & Row.

Hinchman, H. 1997. *A trail through leaves: The journal as a path to place.* New York: W.W. Norton & Company.

hooks, b. 1997. *Wounds of passion: A writing life.* New York: Henry Holt & Company, Inc.

Johnson, D.W., & Johnson, R.T. 1994. *Learning together and alone: Cooperative, competitive, and individualistic learning.* Needham Heights, MA: Allyn and Bacon.

Joyce, B., Weil, M., & Showers, B. 1992. *Models of teaching.* Englewood Cliffs, NJ: Prentice-Hall, Inc.

King, C.S. 1984. *The words of Martin Luther King, Jr.* New York: Newmarket Press.

Kohlberg, L. 1963. The development of children's orientation toward moral order: Sequence in the development of moral thought. *Vita Humana, 6,* 11-33.

Kuhn, T.S. 1970. *The structure of scientific revolutions.* Chicago: University of Chicago Press.

Lezotte, L., Hathaway, D., Miller, S., Passalacqua, J., & Brookover, W. 1980. *School learning climate and school achievement.* Tallahassee, FL: The Site Specific Technical Assistance Center.

Levinson, D.J. 1978. *The seasons of a man's life.* New York: Ballentine.

Lowman, J. 1995. *Mastering the techniques of teaching.* San Francisco: Jossey-Bass, Publishers.

Lopez, B.H. 1986. *Arctic dreams: Imagination and desire in a northern landscape.* New York: Charles Scribner.

Mandela, N. 1994. *Long walk to freedom: The autobiography of Nelson Mandela.* Boston: Little Brown & Co.

Meichenbaum, D., Burland, S., Gruson, L., & Cameron, R. 1985. Meta-cognitive assessment. In S. Yussen (Ed.), *The growth of reflection in children.* Orlando, FL: Academic Press, (pp. 3-30)

Novak, J., & Musonda, D. 1991. A twelve-year longitudinal study of science concept learning. *American Educational Research Journal, 28,* 117-153.

Palmer, P.J. 1998. *The courage to teach: Exploring the inner landscape of a teacher's life.* San Francisco: Jossey-Bass, Publishers.

Patrick, C. 1955. *What is creative thinking?* New York: Philosophical Library.

Perry, W. 1981. Cognitive and ethical growth: The making of meaning. In Chickering, A.W., *The modern American college: Responding to the new realities of diverse students and a changing society.* San Francisco: Jossey-Bass, Publishers, 76-116.

Peters, T.J., & Waterman, R.H. 1982. *In search of excellence: Lessons from American's best-run companies.* New York: Harper & Row.

Peters, T., & Austin, N. 1985. *A passion for excellence: The leadership difference.* New York: Random House.

Peters, T. 1987. *Thriving on chaos: Handbook for a management revolution.* New York: Knopf.

Piaget, J. 1952. *The origins of intelligence in children.* M. Cook (Tr.). New York: International Universities Press.

Rogoff, B. 1990. *Apprenticeship in thinking: Cognitive development in social context.* New York: Oxford University Press.

Sarason, S.B. 1982. *The culture of the school and the problem of change.* Boston: Allyn and Bacon.

Shaheen, R., & Pedrick, W. 1974. *School district climate improvement.* Denver, CO: CFK Limited.

Sheehy, G. 1976. *Passages.* New York: Dutton.

Sheehy, G. 1981. *Pathfinders.* New York: Bantam.

Tharp, R.G., & Gallimore, R. 1988. *Rousing minds to life: Teaching, learning, and schooling in social context..* New York: Cambridge University Press.

Timpson, W.M., Burgoyne, S., Jones, C.S., & Jones, W. 1997. *Teaching and performing: Ideas for energizing your classes.* Madison, WI: Atwood Publishing.

Timpson, W.M., & Bendel-Simso, P. 1996. *Concepts and choices for teaching: Meeting the challenges in higher education.* Madison, WI: Atwood Publishing.

Timpson, W.M, & Broadbent, F. (Eds.). 1995. *Action learning: Experience and promise.* Brisbane, Australia: The University of Queensland's Teaching and Educational Development Institute.

Toffler, A. 1980. *The third wave.* New York: Morrow.

Turnbull, D. 1994. *Maps are territories: Science is an atlas.* Chicago: University of Chicago Press.

Von Oech, R. 1983. *A whack on the side of the head.* New York: Warner.

Von Oech, R. 1986. *A kick in the seat of the pants: Using your explorer, artist, judge and warrior to be more creative.* New York: HarperCollins.